I Miss The Hugs But Not The Hurts

Read what People are saying about this life-changing book!

I Miss the Hugs, But Not the Hurts

"I had put my life on hold for a man, because he promised to change. I didn't have the strength to leave him until I read this book a friend gave me. This book, I Miss the Hugs, But Not the Hurts, ministered to me that I deserved more."

—Alesia Landis, Business Owner, Trenton, Michigan

"It's a book I would read more than once because it's pertinent to different stages of recovery."

—Lisa Parrish, Retired Detroit Police Office, Trenton, Michigan

"The book was excellent! The book ministered to me. It explained why we go through some of the bad relationships we encounter."

—Marlene C.G., Kissimmee, Florida

". . . The book reminded me of my similar mistakes and circumstances with added twists of down to earth frankness that captivated my attention. And by using the Bible as a solution, Dr. Tunishai Ford confirmed how practical the Bible is for our every day lives."

—Minister P.G., Detroit, Michigan

"The book was very educational especially for young women who get caught in different types of relationships looking for love in all the wrong places. It's a great book for those searching for self-respect in their own lives. It's a great guide and a good tool."

—Druesillar Rankins, Human Resource Manager, Chandler, Arizona

"The book was fantastic! It was beautiful, inspiring, and well put. Easy reading. I believe that every woman who reads it will feel the same."

—Diana Gardner, Business Woman, Detroit, Michigan

"This book was outstanding! It changed and saved my life. Before I read this book, I was ready to go back to my abusive ex-husband. This book made me realized that would have destroyed my life.'

—Toni L., Sales Representative, Greenville, Ohio

I Miss The Hugs But Not The Hurts

How to restore, recover, and discover yourself after co-dependency

Dr. Tunishai A. Ford

TATE PUBLISHING
AND ENTERPRISES, LLC

Published by Tate Publishing & Enterprises, LLC
127 E. Trade Center Terrace | Mustang, Oklahoma 73064 USA
1.888.361.9473 | www.tatepublishing.com

Tate Publishing is committed to excellence in the publishing industry. The company reflects the philosophy established by the founders, based on Psalm 68:11,
"The Lord gave the word and great was the company of those who published it."

Published in the United States of America

ISBN: 978-1-62994-913-0
1. Self-Help/Personal Growth/ Self-Esteem
2. Self-Help / Codependency
13.10.09

Dedication

*To the two most
important people in my life: my mother,
Corliss, who has gone to be with the Lord,
and my son, Bayo.*

*Mom, because of your sacrifices and your
undying love for me, you've inspired me to soar
and fly high to reach my full potential.
You are the strongest woman I know and truly you
are the wind beneath my wings.*

*Bayo, you are the reason for my
persistence and drive. I love you with
all my heart and because of your wondrous birth
we became a TEAM. Thank you both for
believing in me and putting your faith in God
to continuously keep me and give me the
ability to live my dream.*

Acknowledgments

I want to first thank and acknowledge my Lord and Savior, Jesus Christ, for giving me the ability and desire to write and for making my dream a reality.

To my friend, Richard Jackson, who has been my backbone through all of my endeavors.

Special thanks to Antoinette Coleman and LaTanya Orr for putting the book together and giving the world the finished product.

To my sister, Rev. Marlene Gingrich-Milarski, for the many prayers and encouragement and unconditional love that you gave me through my greatest trials.
Besides God, I don't think anyone recognizes my gifts and talents and desire to fulfill my purpose as you do.
I love you very much!

Contents

Introduction

When I think back on past relationships, I realize that there were some very valuable lessons learned. Lessons I would like to share with my female counterparts because I believe you are the ones who would greatly benefit the most from those experiences. Although, the majority of the book addresses female issues, I know that the men can appreciate its content. I also devoted a chapter that I hope will be life-changing for the men.

I felt inspired to write this book because of the growing rate of divorce and separation in marriages and the lack of substance in our urban families. The woman and man have lost their desire for commitment. I realize that being in good, healthy relationships is a major factor for happiness and feeling completeness in one's life. But, unfortunately, many people will not recognize this to be true. Many go through their lives never experiencing the beauty of true love and its many splendors.

Now, let me clarify my statement on feeling completeness. By no means am I trying to imply that one must have a mate to be a whole person. I am merely saying that when a healthy relationship is in existence, people can experience an additional factor to their happiness, which makes them feel more complete.

The famous psychologist, Abraham Maslow, understood that there are basic needs in our lives that are necessary to our existence. Guess what? Sex is not one of them, but the presence of love is very pertinent for our overall being. How often, though, is it the acts of sex that so many place emphasis upon? In fact, upon entering into a relationship with the opposite sex, both genders anticipate when the first sexual encounter will occur. If it takes too long, the assumption that love could be blossoming might very well be dismissed.

It is my intent to address the issues that both hinder and create healthy relationships, and encourage women to strive to obtain that completeness without continually experiencing the pitfalls of relationships. Whether you are a veteran in the field of love or a first-timer, this book is for you. If you are in a platonic relationship with the same sex and you want to know what components are important for a healthy, fulfilling friendship—I believe this book is for you. You don't have to compromise your happiness and well-being to have a relationship with anyone. Love was intended to bring happiness into our lives, not heartache and resentment. I am saddened that the most beautiful force that God created has been tainted and destroyed by so many who have turned their obsession into lust, and love can very seldom be found.

In this book, I'm going to get real with you and there will be no sugar-coating. When I wrote the first version, I was real light. I didn't want to get too raw because it was my first book and I really didn't have a clear and precise vision for the book. Now my vision is crystal clear and I'm on a mission. I'm going to attack the lies that have deceived so many people and have placed barriers that hinder us from reaching our full potential. I want to help restore hope and dreams to those who understand that true love covers a multitude of faults. Love is the only force that allows us to reach our goals without wrongly compromising. This book is intended to reach everyone. I'm not exclusively writing to the church nor am I writing to appease the world. The message is for those who have an ear to hear the truth and embrace it with a conviction to do something different without allowing themselves to succumb to the temptations that they will later regret.

Everyone deserves to be loved and to love whether you serve God or not. My desire is that everyone comes into the knowledge of the truth. Because I am a minister, my desire is to point you to God and to encourage you to serve Him wholeheartedly as it is His desire, but let's get real with this thing. It's not going to happen, if we loose the desire to respect and honor the institution of love. So first things first, I'm trying to combat some of this madness and point those who don't have a clue about true love in the right direction. Those who have become disillusioned about it, I want to give them a new sense of hope and belief. Any man or woman should expect the best out of life; having a healthy and loving relationship should be just as important as having the fine homes and cars, and fulfilling your dreams.

Stop the madness! Strive to be a better person. Don't give yourself to every Tom, Dick, Harry and Sally who gives you a smooth line. "If you love me, you will allow me to mess up your life." This is what's in the hearts of so many people whom we allow to get close to us and don't have good intentions. It's time to start making the right choices and stand alone for a minute to get ourselves together. You can do this even if it means giving up the hugs to get rid of the hurts. You can do it!

Lord, Why Do I Keep Attracting the Wrong Men?

O kay ladies; let's take a look at what I call a 'Slam Bam' situation. Now, here you are, you have got it going on for yourself. In addition to being very attractive, you have a decent paying job, you are buying your home, and you drive a nice vehicle. You do not consider yourself to be conceited, but let's face it, ladies, you have worked hard to get where you are, and someone coming into your life with the intention of using you is not going to sit well. Here he is; no job nor education and not trying to get one or is making minimum wage with no aspirations. He does not own a vehicle, but he always wants to ride in one or borrow yours. His place of residence is wherever he can lay his head on, preferably in your bed.

By this time, you are wondering who would allow themselves to get into this kind of situation. Over thirty percent of the women in America are in relationships with men who offer nothing more than a heavy load to carry. These men are very needy and they have no problem with needing YOU!

These men often come into your life with baggage and have unresolved issues such as drug, alcohol or gambling addictions

They are in debt up to their heads and the Friend of the Court has submitted their pictures and profiles to the America's Most Wanted deadbeat fathers' list. Not to mention, many of these men have excessive anger, controlling, jealousy, and possessiveness problems. Oh, and let's not forget the most popular one, the baby's mama drama. Girl, are you feeling me?

This is a situation I found myself in, many times. It bothered me when men like these were attracted to me. Now I know it is flattering to be admired and desired, but if you are not in the market for an under-educated smoker and drinker, run and run fast.

After this happened to me, I began to examine my actions, my body language and my conversations; because I truly wanted to know what I was doing to draw these men to me. It saddened me that these kind of men thought they could have me because I was willing to settle for them. I was not strong enough to wait for the best for my life.

Sometimes there is a mutual attraction. They know what they are getting but you do not know what you have walked into. This is the situation I found myself in; compromising and lowering my standards became all too familiar just because I wanted to have someone in my life.

In the past, I allowed myself to get involved with one of my students. At that time, I was a new teacher in the Adult Education system. A respected, moral, religious, and giving leader in Detroit opened a school named Calnet. I accepted a job there, leaving a very comfortable position where I was counseling and conducting empowerment workshops for students of the EDGE program. I was assigned a teaching position for ABE/GED grammar. I was not a happy camper, but I had a thirteen-year-old son to support, so I went without protest to my new assignment.

What I am about to disclose is not something that I am proud of, but this experience was one that taught me a valuable lesson. It gave me the conviction and self-respect that I needed to share the knowledge that I am presently conveying in this book.

The program was brand new and I wanted so much to enjoy what I was assigned to do. I made a real effort to make my class very interesting. Because I have the gift of gab, it was not unusual to find me motivating my students and sharing my life experiences with them. They let their hair down because I let my hair down. My desire was to make the classroom fun and interesting. Because of my outgoing personality and openness, I believe I attracted the attention of a few of my male students. But there was one in particular that I became attracted to. His name was Donny. Donny was suave, intelligent, well groomed, handsome, and, of course, without a high school diploma.

I was immediately attracted to him, and I must also mention that I thought he was a spiritual man. In fact, he was everything I wanted in a man—minus the house, the job, the education; the proper English, the ambition, the . . . Hey, are you beginning to get the picture?

This man was FINE, but this man would never be the proper soul mate for me because his past life was still a crippling part of his life, and he was not about to let that go. At the same time, Donny was a worldly man and had a background filled with addictions. Although he was trying to change, his past continued to haunt him, even down to his ex-girlfriend.

We began to see each other outside the school setting. Thank God we both had enough sense to be discreet about the relationship! I believe the areas of interest that made me draw closer to him were his spiritual convictions. He really appeared to love God and seemed to be thirsty for all the knowledge he could learn about Him. We would talk for hours about life. Because he was seven years my senior, he had a lot about life to share. I became so intrigued with his knowledge and past life that I didn't have a problem becoming the pupil.

As I write these words, I think about the memories that now occupy just a small part of my mind. At the time, my world evolved around this man and all I could think about was being with him. I was actually considering being with this man, even though I knew our backgrounds were quite different and this man was not educated. It didn't appear that the GED was going to be a part of his future anytime soon.

Somebody please SLAP ME! These were the words I uttered when our relationship became nothing but ongoing arguments, because we eventually could no longer see eye-to-eye. As earlier mentioned, the ex-girlfriend was in the picture and his heart was always there with her. But I was the new thang; therefore, I was exciting and intriguing to him. He wanted to have his cake and eat it too!

He managed to spend time with both of us while he became so entangled in his web of confusion. I was in a triangle and I knew it was time to get out. Although I was very attracted to him, my mind and heart told me that this man was not for me. His ex had nothing to do with my apprehension. The lack of common denominators was the largest factor on my mind. I was concerned that misery would forever be my constant companion, and I was not about to let that happen.

Are you a glutton for punishment? This question may be going through your head right about now. No, I am not, but the saying that my mother taught me kind of sums up what I, and other women who fall into this trap, experience. My mother always said that, Loneliness makes strange friends and strange bedfellows. I dare say that ladies, you also have settled at one point in your lives. They may not have been total degenerates, but you felt that somewhere along the line, you could have done better.

I thought that I had learned my lesson, but it happened a second and several times after that; which brings me to the next story. Because of having respect for the privacy of the men I was involved with, I won't use their real names. Now allow me to tell you about a man that I actually became engaged to. I will call him Lee. He was a minister-in-training and he was extremely faithful to his local church. When we met, he was very charming and appeared to be very sincere in his intentions. He had one major problem though—he was a cocaine addict with just a few months of sobriety under his belt. He had just completed a treatment program when we met.

When he approached me, my first mind was to not get involved with this person because I knew that he lacked many of the qualities

I desired and felt should be present in a man. Also, I had no business getting involved with anyone who had a drug addiction. Of course, he was very persistent, and he and I often shared our thoughts and feelings about spiritual issues. He had a lot of wisdom. I must admit his wisdom was definitely an attractive quality to me. I was introduced to his church and they immediately welcomed me with open arms. Again, I was quite impressed with this feature in his life because I was seeking a new church home.

We began to fellowship on a regular basis. He treated me like a queen. He opened doors for me and would bring me flowers. There was nothing he would not do for me. I also became very involved with the church. In fact, the pastor asked me to start an empowerment class for the women. On Thursday evenings, I taught the women and the pastor taught the men. I was elated and felt like I really belonged somewhere again.

My relationship was coming along, but I began to see the negative traits that confirmed my reservations about him. He was extremely jealous. He would accuse me of liking both his best friend and the church's pastor. He was controlling and very possessive. My nightmare had begun; he was constantly accusing and displaying anger.

As the relationship progressed, he went back to his first love—crack cocaine. When we initially started talking, he told me he had completed six to eight months of sobriety time and he was finished with those past-life habits. I believed him, but I had some reservations that were undoubtedly confirmed. He fell, not one time, but several times. That last time was the one that almost cost me my life.

I lowered my standards because Lee convinced me that he was going to try to better himself. I was lonely and didn't want to go through another summer alone. I became an enabler because I didn't want to let go, although in my heart, I knew this relationship would never last.

I had many opportunities to walk away from this relationship, but my desire to be in a relationship was so strong that it overtook my sense of sound reasoning.

Ladies, how many of you have been in a bad relationship and you were so involved that you did not know how to walk away? For me, there was a sense of helplessness, because there was quite a strong connection between us; it was a soul tie. I really didn't believe I could break away, although I knew I needed to do just that.

This brings me to my newfound conviction. I do not want to come across as being judgmental, but this story is not only common to me, in fact it is too common. Talk show hosts are making millions on this plight, and many of them probably go home and laugh about it to their families and friends. On the TV court shows, the matters are mainly about relationships that have gone wrong. Again, the judges are probably in their chambers laughing about how foolish the couples are on the show. Why do we allow ourselves to be victims? What possesses us to go out and play the part of an idiot? Now, I know that's a very strong word and may be offensive, but I am really making an effort to make a point here. The word idiot is defined as 'having a mental deficiency and not being able to function beyond the mentality of a four-year-old.'

Some of us have made decisions in our lives that reflect that there was very little brain activity taking place. When I reflected back on my decisions, I realized that I had brought that on myself and I didn't think at all. I consider myself to be an intelligent woman, but I thought with my heart, not my brain. You are probably thinking to yourself right about now that I am being hard on others and myself. Okay, think about it. The human body is very complex. God made it that way for a reason. I am sure that He made the brain to think reasonably and responsibly, and the heart to bring a conviction or confirmation to the decision that the mind makes. In our society, in many instances, the brain is vacationing and the heart and the sexual organs have taken over when it comes down to getting involved in a serious relationship. In fact, that is the problem. The seriousness does not take precedence in our decision-making because the primary focus often times is on sex, not love and commitment.

This sexual freedom that is being displayed is creating a lot of social problems such as a high rate in teenage pregnancies and AIDS, along with other STDs. Every time we read the magazines or look at the news, we see many celebrities going in and out of relationships. The divorce rate is higher among Christians than it has ever been, and infidelity is so common now that it has become a household name. Trust me when I tell you this, there is no sexual freedom. You are going to pay a grave price! We have to stop this madness and get back to the ways of God. Desire to be with one partner for a lifetime in marriage.

Make a commitment to work on your issues in your relationships before you decide to throw it all away. I wish that I could make everyone see what I see. The revelation that God has given me is profound. He knows that we have sexual desires. Guess what? He gave them to us. Sex is powerful! Nations have been destroyed because of sexual indiscretions; families and communities have been broken up because of it. Sex is the main force that Satan has used to deceive and separate us. If we would come to the realization that this is hindering us and not helping us we could overcome and defeat this enemy. Don't misunderstand me. I am not saying that sex is a bad thing, but I am saying that for the most part, sex, which was created to be beautiful and shared between two committed people, has been perverted and is responsible for many of the spiritual, social, and economical issues that we face today. Now I want to get back to my experience with Lee.

The last time he gave in to his addiction was the straw that broke the camel's back. This man not only assaulted me physically, he scarred me emotionally, psychologically, and spiritually. I came very close to losing my life and also the respect and admiration of my son. Lee came back to my home after going out to 'use'. He returned around midnight. He rang the doorbell and I knew, I shouldn't have let him in. We had an argument earlier that day and he stormed out of the house and didn't return until late that evening. He demanded money from me and I told him I did not have any. I did have money in the house, but that was money that I put aside for the wedding. He was full of rage and he had a look on his face that I had never seen before. I could actually see the demon that was driving him. He insisted that I give him money and when I refused, he shoved me onto the couch and tried to smother me with a couch pillow. I somehow broke away from him and ran into the bedroom. He was very well built and I could not handle him physically. He pushed me down on the bed and placed his hands around my neck and the look in his eyes let me know that this was not the man I knew—but a sickness, a demon, a great evil force that did not care about me. It just wanted to feed that cocaine hunger no matter what it cost. I called out his name several times hoping that he would come to his senses and all of a sudden I saw a look of regret come over his face. He let me up and proceeded to go into the other bedroom. He looked under the dresser and found the box in which I had placed the money and he took it. It was over $400.00 and he took it all.

Before all of this happened, about a week earlier, I prayed and asked God to help me and show me what to do about this man. I was making wedding plans and I was so unhappy. All of my friends could see that there was not joy in my heart and they continued to ask me why I was doing it. I felt trapped! I did not know how to get out. I cried out to God and asked Him to get me out of this hopeless situation. Needless to say, He heard my prayer and on that night when Lee left my home for the last time, God asked me, "IS IT CLEAR NOW?" It was very clear and as I sat on my bed collecting by life back, I realized how serious this was and how God really intervened. I sobbed and called a friend and told her what happened to me and then I waited for my son to come home to let him know what happened. I also called the pastor and he talked me out of calling the police. I regret that decision now, but I did not call them, and to this day Lee is still using drugs, and I know he is very unhappy and feeling guilty about what he did to me. I guess you can say that he is paying for his sin.

The most difficult part of my ordeal was facing my son and trying to explain to him why his mother would allow herself to get involved with someone who was not on my intellectual, spiritual, and economic level, and not to mention, also a drug addict. When my son found me lying on the couch in a state of shock, he asked me what happened and when I proceeded to tell him, the look on his face made me feel so humiliated. I was ashamed that my son had to know that his mother was so weak. My only concern was my son's feelings about me from that day forward.

We need to understand that the decisions we make are not just affecting us. They affect our loved ones as well, especially our children. Some of you may think that because you are the parent, it does not matter what your children think or say. On the contrary, those bad relationships that they see you going in and out of, can greatly influence them and affect their outlook and future decisions they make when choosing a companion.

God delivered me from that situation. Although there was hurt and disappointment, there was also joy and peace. Even if he was on my educational, financial, social, and spiritual level, and did not have an addiction; the mere fact that he was controlling, and had an anger and jealousy problem, would have been reason enough to destroy the relationship.

Many of you who are reading this book may be saying to yourselves, this does not apply to me. So what, if he is not where I am in some areas! Let's be honest. You are settling, and nine times out of ten, he is going to bring you down to his level. Very seldom will you bring him up to yours. No one wants to be alone, but it is not God's will that you should spend your time being miserable with anyone either. The most beautiful forms of God's creation were man and woman. He intended for the two to become one, joined in love and companionship, not control or entrapment.

If you are in a relationship today, and you know that he is not what you want, trust God to give you the courage to GET OUT. If you are in a relationship just for the sex, you are making the worse mistake of your life. Abstinence is not going to kill you. In fact it will probably save you. No one has ever gotten pregnant or contracted a STD by abstaining from sex. When you use your body solely as a sexual tool, you cheat yourself out of a fulfilling and wonderful experience of knowing true and committed love. Hey, let's do this thing right. If you have to be alone for a while, do so and make the best of it. Take the time alone to get to know the greatest person in the world—YOU! Learn to respect the person you are and the person you desire to become. Do this for YOU!

He who goes out weeping, carrying seed
to sow, will return with songs of joy, carrying
sheaves with him (Psalm 126:6, NIV).

"My mother always said,
'Loneliness makes strange friends
and strange bedfellows.'"

Chapter One
Questions to Consider

1. Reflect on your past or present relationships and ask yourself what attracted you to this person? Make a list. Now be honest with yourself.

2. How long did you stay in a relationship that you knew you were unhappy in and why?

3. Are you still with that person? If not, what compelled you to leave?

4. Are you ready to release the hurts of past and present relationships? If you are, recite this prayer:

"Father,
in the name of Jesus. I come to you
asking for forgiveness for allowing myself to
get involved with the wrong person. I was
anxious and didn't wait on you to send that
perfect helpmate for me. I ask that you
cleanse me and give me a fresh start.
Allow me to guard my heart and
stay focused on the things you placed in
my heart to do. Thank you Father,
Amen."

Respect Yourself

R.E.S.P.E.C.T. These are the letters that Aretha Franklin sings out on her hit record. In her song, it is all about giving her respect. But if she has to demand it, then she was doing something wrong, or she obviously chose the WRONG one.

First things first: Respect yourself. Respecting yourself comes from having a positive, healthy and loving relationship with you. Yes! You can have a relationship with yourself. Think about it. You spend more time with yourself than with anyone else in your life. It makes sense that respect should be self-given before you expect anyone else to respect you. One of the areas I find that many women lack respect for themselves, is in their appearance.

For many of you sisters, the flesh must be showing in order for you to feel good about yourselves. Even you full-figured women have to let it all hang out! It is insulting to see how these women display themselves to men as a cheap piece of meat. Somebody told you that this was sexy and you believed it. A woman who truly has herself together knows that her sexuality is based on a strong spiritual bond between her and her lover (or husband) and not flaunting her stuff before every man she runs across to obtain validation. Sexy is what God made it. It is for the marriage bed where it is honored and respected. It is in that arena that the woman can truly express herself to her man without conviction and negative consequences. There is no shame in her game. Being sexy is when your man knows every area of your body that excites you and you can freely respond to his touches and kisses without inhibition. We have allowed that which is ungodly, to dictate to us and set our standards for us. As a result of this dictation, many have fallen prey to this web of destruction. Respect is not based on what is showing on the outside; it comes from what is on the inside that is displayed on the outside. That is who you are! Your clothes should reflect who you are on the inside, and if in your outer appearance, your display to others shows the lack of self-respect, there are many who will be eager to show you just that—little or no respect.

We are also living in a time where sex is used to promote and even illustrate a behavior that suggests a lack of moral fiber. It appears that our society does not see anything wrong with the practice of too many sexual partners. Women are having babies out of wedlock and they do not know who the father is, but if you ask them if they respect themselves, they will tell you that they do. Maybe something is wrong with my thinking, but having more than one sexual partner within the same time frame, and allowing your body to be used and misused is not having respect for yourself . . . and guess what? He does not respect you either. Why should he?

Again, our sexuality is a gift that God has given us to express love to one partner—our spouses. By the time marriage is brought into the picture, the number of sexual partners we have had can go into the tens, twenties, or even hundreds. Now I know what you are thinking. You are probably thinking to yourselves right now that you have only been with a few men, but allow me to give you a revelation. Every woman he slept with, you slept with; and every man you slept with, he slept with. Therefore, every sexual partner you both had is shared among all of your partners. You became one flesh with everyone you slept with. So you see, you had multiple partners although you may have only had the pleasure of actually laying with a few partners.

Then the Lord God made a woman from the rib he had
taken out of the man, and he brought her to the man.
The man said, "This is now bone of my bones and flesh
of my flesh; she shall be called 'woman' for she was
taken out of man. "For this reason a man will leave his
father and mother and be united to his wife, and they
will become one flesh (Genesis 2: 22-24, NIV).

Being a minister, I am obligated to express to you how God feels about this matter. In 1 Corinthians 7:1-9, God states that sex outside of the marriage is not His will and is a sin. There are serious consequences to having illicit sex. He says that everyone who desires to have sex should marry, and they should engage in sexual relationships with their own spouse. I am a true believer that there is only one voice of reason in the world and that is God's. He created man and He created sex, love and marriage—not in that order—but that is often man's order. It makes sense to me that since He created man, He would know better than anyone what actually makes us tick. It is amazing to me that man actually believes his opinion is the authority on the matter. God has given man a small glimpse of a very large picture, and we have taken it and ran with it.

Now for the matters you wrote about: it is good
for a man not to marry, but since there is so much
immorality, each man should have his own wife,
and each woman her own husband
(1 Corinthians 7: 1, 2, NIV).

When we understand this concept, we will develop a group of guidelines for getting into a relationship, platonic or otherwise. I believe that there should be some criteria that an individual should meet before allowing one to become emotionally and physically involved. Let us take a look at a couple:

Having a Similar Value System. You do not have to think like I think, but your value system should not put you at the top of

America's Most Wanted. Right is right and wrong is wrong. You should at least have similar values that would help develop the stability of a relationship.

Too many times we are guilty of being unequally yoked. Being unequally yoked does not apply only to the spiritual area, but to every other area as well. If I have very strong spiritual convictions (which I do), and I am in a relationship with someone who does not possess strong spiritual convictions, do not think for a moment that our relationship will not be affected by the lack of compatibility in this area. Spiritual compatibility is just one area that can greatly affect a relationship. Other areas include our outlook on raising children, money manageability and sexual openness, just to name a few. Of course, no one is going to be perfectly compatible with you in every area, but make sure your differences are not so extreme that you compromise and sacrifice your happiness for another individual. To do so is truly a lack of respect for you.

Allow me to share with you another situation I got myself into. I told you how I was always attracting the wrong guy, right? Well here is another one. I will call him Wayne. Now Wayne was also a cutie pie. He was slim and trimmed, and fair skinned with nice hair. Get the picture? Oh, and did I mention homeless (laugh)! I know what you are thinking. Where did I find these guys? Well I found Wayne at a drug rehabilitation center. Wayne was an alcoholic. He was charming at first and had the most beautiful smile. Hey, I was a sucker for a beautiful smile. He attracted me because he loved to dress nicely and was always well-groomed. He was going to school to obtain his GED, and he was also part of the ministry at the center he lived in. My attraction to Wayne was definitely a physical one, and we had nothing else going for us in this relationship. Although he was attractive, he acted very ugly. He took every opportunity he could find to put me down, and we did not have similar values either. He did not even treat me like I was special to him. I would allow him to drive my vehicle. Of course I would be with him, and he did not even want to open the door for me. The only time he would treat me to a meal would be whenever he could recall me treating him the last time. This went on for at least three to five months. I was tired of the verbal abuse and the constant degrading comments that came out of his mouth, but he was a man that only had one thing going for himself—a few clothes, which were probably second-hand items. We were definitely incompatible in many areas, but I stayed with this man as long as I did because I was attracted to him. Does this sound familiar ladies? Yes, it does. Let us be for real.

Many of you are with a man right now because of a physical attraction and there is nothing else happening. You have talked yourselves into believing that his appearance was enough to keep the love flowing or you tell yourself you truly see something else in him that you admire. Girl, please. Let it go!! If you are in a situation that I just described, you are not respecting that fine sister that you look at everyday in the mirror. You have to know that you are better than that. Set your standards higher and do not let them go. Come on now, be realistic. Do not expect something from a man that you are not, but do not go and scrap the bottom of the barrel either.

Similar Expectations for the Relationship. Another area that we should be critical about when choosing a companion or a platonic friend is whether or not both parties view the relationship in the same manner. In other words, do you both have the same expectations for the relationship?

Let me expound upon this. Many years ago, I had a friend of whom I grew to be very fond. I thought she felt the same way about me. We always talked on the phone and spent a lot of time together. We shared a lot of intimate and deeply felt thoughts with each other. I believed the relationship was moving along fine. One day, during one of our conversations, I expressed how much I cherished her as a friend and how much I wanted her to be a big part of my life. Well, she dropped a bomb on me and politely told me that she was not interested in a friendship. She just wanted someone to talk to and hang out with, every now and then. I must say that I was extremely hurt and disappointed. I was not only feeling rejected, but quite embarrassed. Although this was just a platonic relationship, we both had different expectations

Please, do not misunderstand me. By no means am I trying to imply that she did anything wrong. I am merely saying that she did not want a deeper friendship and that was fine.

Now the same is also true in a non-platonic relationship or as it is often called, a romantic one. I cannot begin to tell you how many times I had higher expectations for a relationship than the man's. It often left me broken-hearted and depressed. Who was I kidding? I wanted to be married and every man I became involved with was supposed to be a potential mate. This goes on all the time, especially among church folk. We know that sex outside of marriage is a no-no and we want to justify why we are DOING IT! We go to God with this lame line and tell Him that we fell and we could not get up. So please let him be the one. Make him right for me, oh Lord. Oh, I am sorry! That only happened to me? I know that anyone reading this book has never been guilty of this action, right?

Ladies, this is happening all the time. I told you earlier that I was going to be real with you because this has to stop. If a man wants to be in a committed relationship, he will ask you. You do not have to give up the bootie to get him. If you are with someone who's telling you very clearly that he is not ready for marriage or he just wants a play toy, listen to him. He is telling you how it is laying. He did not stutter; he said it loud and clear. So if the man is telling you that his mind is not on marriage and your mind is on the subject, you need to be looking for the nearest exit. Stop blaming him for stringing you along. You have placed yourself in this web, now you get yourself out.

It took a man to tell me that I was foolish. It took him to point out to me how much time and energy I wasted going after men who did not want what I wanted. I was always the one bringing up marriage and it scared them. They may have liked me a lot, but I was literally pushing them away. There are many men who are really ready to be in a loving, committed relationship, but even they, want to be the ones who bring up the subject. My friend told me not to ever bring up the subject of marriage to a man. He said that if the man's intentions were honorable, then he would ask me to marry him. He also told me not to stay in a relationship too long waiting for it to happen either. What is too long you ask? Years and years and years.

I have heard how some couples have been together for ten years and they are no closer to the altar than the day they met. Many women do not see anything wrong with that. They have convinced themselves that this is all right, and will curse anyone out if they pointed out to them that they did not have anything going for themselves in the relationship. Unless they live in a state where common law marriages are recognized, if that man dies, they get nothing. Please do not let the man have children, because then they get double nothing. In other words . . . I will let you finish the sentence.

Self-respect is deep and it has many factors. Most of us probably set our own standards for what we call self-respect and I guess that is okay if you really think you have got it going on like that. Just remember that when it comes down to you, if it is hurting and uncomfortable, then it needs to be re-examined. Also, if it affects the lives of your children negatively, then something is wrong too. Self-respect is not geared to please other people all the time, but we should make sure that our actions are not morally offensive and will not cause danger to others in the long run. When entering a new relationship, especially when you feel drawn to an individual, it is best to talk about expectations and what the relationship means to both of you. Some might say, well, just let things happen. Yes, things can just happen, but remember, your time is very valuable. Do not wait forever. If the other person is only in it for a ride, and will be getting off shortly at the next stop, do not expect them to conform to your dream of a lifetime partner. Listen to them and take them very seriously. If and when they decide to change the relationship, and you still desire to take it to another level, they will let you know.

Okay, by now you are probably asking yourself what do these criteria have to do with respecting yourself. Well, ask yourself, are you a glutton for punishment? Why would you want to be in a relationship with anyone when you are unfulfilled? It is okay if a person does not want to get close to you, but it is not okay if you want more from a relationship and you are not getting it. YOU do not have to settle for less if you sincerely want more. Do not compromise your values, beliefs and desires to please someone else. When you begin to be true to yourself and not lower your standards just to have companionship, you will be operating in one of the greatest elements of love—Self-Respect.

God made us to be social beings, and if He intended for mankind to dwell alone, He would have given us all our own private little islands. All we would do all day would be to look up at the sky and curse God for giving us such a bleak existence. He said in the beginning that we were not meant to be alone (Genesis 2:18). God, being all knowing and all sufficient, recognized that He, alone, would not be enough for mankind. He wanted us to love and be loved by enjoying the pleasures of sharing our lives with others through the institution of marriage, the communion of family, the company of friends, and the splendor of romance.

Self-respect will eventually draw all of these things to you. It is inevitable that a healthy and fulfilling relationship will come your way. People will begin to recognize and appreciate the confidence that you exude. Self-respect is a very powerful drawing force. When you continue to walk in it, you will find that you will not be walking alone. Self-respect is the integrity of the soul. It initiates the presence of a positive self-image. Without it, hurt and disappointments will be your constant companion because you have allowed yourself to be trapped by the negativity and poison of others who do not respect themselves and are, therefore incapable of respecting you.

Self-respect will guide you and be your conscience for every relationship that you may encounter. But if we do not possess it, we will find ourselves singing a rendition of Aretha

Franklin's song, R.E.S.P.E.C.T. I promise you; it will not win you a Grammy.

I believe that self-respect comes from being taught that you are worthy to have good things in your life. Unfortunately, many people have not been taught this valuable lesson. It should start at home as children with our parents, but in our society many of the parents are not living exemplary lives before their children. The children do not see parents respecting themselves so there is nothing to emulate. Especially our girls, they need their mothers to be their role models. When they see their mothers taking up time with any old thing, and she's allowing the man to abuse her and live common law around the child, how is the child supposed to learn self-respect when the first role model of her life is 'jacked up.' Our children's lives are being destroyed because of premarital sex and pregnancy. They do not know any better.

> My people are destroyed from lack of knowledge,
> (Hosea 4:6, NIV).

> Train a child in the way he should go, and when he is
> old he will not turn from it,
> (Proverbs 22: 6, NIV).

It is never too late to learn to respect yourself. Sometimes that lesson does have to come from the school of hard knocks. It does not matter how we learn it, as long as we learn it. For self-respect will not guarantee that you will not fall into the pitfalls of 'pseudo love' too often. I did not say you will not ever fall, but your feet will not have a chance to make an imprint because you will not be staying there too long. In the meantime, do not lower your standards or compromise your beliefs just to be in a relationship with anyone. Respecting yourself does not happen overnight. Because we have experienced so many unpleasant events in our lives, we have been stripped of the ability to care about ourselves the way we should. But when we come to the realization that our self-worth does not come from the validation of man, but the validation of God, then and only then will self respect come. The relationship we have with ourselves and God will stay front and centered. And, if you can believe that God, who is perfect, loves you, then you can believe you are worthy of being loved and that is the greatest love of all.

> I will give you a new heart and put a new spirit in
> you; I will remove from you your heart of stone and
> give you a heart of flesh (Ezekiel 36:26, NIV).

"Because we have experienced so many unpleasant events in our lives, we have been stripped of the ability to care about ourselves the way we should. But when we come to the realization that our self-worth does not come from the validation of man, but the validation of God, then and only then will self-respect come."

Chapter 2
Questions to Consider

1. What is respect? Can you honestly say that you respect yourself?

2. Do other people respect you? Identify the reasons you believe they do or don't.

3. Respect is earned—what are you doing to ensure that you continually earn respect or not earn respect?

4. How does God f eel about self-respect? See if you can find a scripture that supports how he feels about self-respect.

C H A P T E R   T H R E E

Can You Stand To Be Alone?

"I am tired of being alone!" These were the words that I had often heard myself and other single women say with so much despair in our hearts. Loneliness had been my constant companion for years. This is why I allowed myself to become entangled in bad relationships. It was the spring and summer seasons that tripped me up all of the time. I could deal with the holidays because they were just one day each, but oh, the spring and summer were very difficult for me to endure alone. It was warm and all the couples would come out and you could just sense love in the air. Romance was calling my name and I had a hard time resisting it. In fact, most of the men that I became involved with I met during the warm months. I was weak and I admit it. If they came within the 'half way decent line' during those warm months, I was more than likely going to fall for them.

Frankly, I just grew weary of feeling like a statistic. My daily thoughts were about having someone special in my life. I began having headaches and very anxious feelings because I allowed these thoughts to virtually consume me. I could feel myself beginning to deteriorate physically, mentally, and spiritually. Yet, I knew that there had to be someone who could rescue me from my frustration.

Enough was enough. I could not continue life in the same mode. I did not want to continue attracting the wrong men. I wanted this escapade to stop. So one evening I cried out to God and told Him that I was tired of carrying this burden, and I was going to give it to Him totally and completely. I realized at that moment that being anxious about it was not going to bring a companion to me any sooner. It only opened a wider door for the counterfeit to get in. That is right; when you exude that kind of energy, it attracts negative forces.

Don't you realize that the wrong man can sense when you are vulnerable and anxious? There are men who deliberately seek out women who are in that state of mind. These are the women in the homeless shelters, drug rehabilitation centers, abusive marriages, who allow themselves to have multiple sex partners and not know who the fathers of their children are. These are the women who are educated and seemingly got it going on, and the man they are with is married, and somehow he has convinced her that he is going to leave his wife of twenty years for her. These are the women who are the socialites. They sport themselves with a younger man just for the sex, but deep inside they wish just for once they could meet someone that would love them for them, and not for what they have or what they can give him. These are the women who cannot stand to be alone! I believe I described many of us and if you were one of those women I described, then just place your name in this space_____. This space is for you. Do not worry. I have already put my name in that space. So I am not judging. I have pointed the finger at myself so many times and I am tired now. I realized that it was time to release and let God. Now I implore you to do the same if you are the woman in the space or the one I described.

Soon after I released this burden, something wonderful happened. I felt a resurrection; a new beginning. A sudden joy and peace came over me, and at that moment I realized that I would be all right. Also, I came to the conclusion that during this time of aloneness, it would be the perfect time to work on ME. I discovered that being alone was a good thing and I was okay with it. That was the best time to work on some short term and long term goals, and working on myself would be the perfect solution to fill the void in my life. I could take that time and really work on bettering myself and appreciating my wholeness.

Preparation is not lost time, are the words that came to mind as I felt a new excitement for my life. Believing that life could be fulfilling without someone right now, I was beginning to feel very comfortable. I actually felt relieved that I did not get tied up with the wrong man. That meant that there was still hope and room for God to send the right one. Ladies there is still hope! That is something to shout about. I decided that I was going to work on my self-image and getting my vision for becoming an empowerment/personal improvement trainer off the ground.

I have a business/ministry called YOUR OWN UNIQUENESS, Inc. This is a nonprofit organization whose mission is to help women and youth reach their full potential based on Godly principles. In 2001, I became incorporated and in 2002 I received my 501(C)3 status. I am in the process of getting my staff in place and implementing my program. I have also finished my second book entitled, *THIS IS A COMMA IN YOUR LIFE, NOT A PERIOD.* This is a book about my battle and triumph over cancer. Devoting my energies in these areas alone would be very time consuming and, not to mention, very fulfilling.

It is God's perfect will for everyone to have a soul mate, but unfortunately, He does not give us this soul mate when we snap our fingers. In fact, the wait may appear to be an eternity. You are often left feeling like He has forgotten about you. As I have often felt. I cannot explain to you why your best friend has a husband and you do not, or why all of your single friends are involved in these wonderful relationships that you can only dream about. You may even find yourself feeling envious and unable to share in your friends' happiness, but those feelings are not abnormal. It is normal to feel left out sometimes and even question why it has not happened for you yet. I am forty-eight years old and for the life of me, I do not understand why I am still alone. I honestly do not have the energy anymore to dwell on it. I want a companion. I would be lying if I told you that I no longer desire a husband but I want to make sure that my life is in order first. I want to give him the best possible me that I can give him, and I hope that who ever he is, he desires the same.

I have many friends who are married and they have it all. To look at the outside, they are living the American dream, fine homes and cars, good paying jobs and husbands; husbands that they would have gladly done without if they could do it all again. At one time in my life I was very envious of one friend because I looked at her as 'having it all.' I was always comparing myself to her and never seeming to measure up. I was miserable. She had everything I thought until one day I took a real close look. I looked too close I believe and discovered that she just had things with no substance. The elements in life that really mattered, she did not possess at all. She felt she did not have the admiration and adoration from her spouse. She only had things and she got exactly what she expected. I recall before she married her husband, I asked her why she was going to marry him. You know, just girl talk, and she told me the most amazing thing. She said she was marrying him because they could obtain things together and then she added that she loved him, but she never said that she thought that he would be a good father to her (then) small children or a loving, caring companion to her. As it turned out, the father that her now grown children needed, and the loving, caring companion she desired, he couldn't become. They are still together and they have the things but there is so much missing in this ideal, American dream family. I do not envy her anymore, and even if everything were perfect in her life, I would not envy her because I have learned that happiness will come to me in its own time. I will focus on making myself happy as I utilize this time to grow and discover things about me.

You may know people that seemingly have it all together r really do have it all together, but they are not you. Do not waste your time and energy focusing on them. It is human nature to sometimes envy someone because of his or her good fortune. However, you do not want to waddle in it, because it can become toxic and hinder your opportunity for happiness.

I learned that when we allow envy to come in, it is because we do not believe that something similar can happen for us. Envy, jealousy, and comparing ourselves with others are merely symptoms of low self-worth; and it is this reason that you believed that having good things come your way is not for you.

For years, I struggled with these symptoms of low self-worth. They continued to haunt me until I began to fight back. How was I ever going to come to a place of contentment if I was constantly battling with these demons? Because my self-esteem was so low, I took up with men who I knew were beneath me. I guess in a way this was my solution to helping me feel better about myself. I did not think that the educated guys would want me or I just was not attractive and smart enough for them. I believed that by going with these other men that were not on my level actually made me feel better about myself. That may sound like sick therapy, but think about it. It is human nature to place ourselves on a pedestal when we can compare ourselves to something of lesser value.

As I stated earlier in this chapter, when I made up my mind to, 'let go and let God' I knew that giving it over was not going to be the final solution. It was a big and pertinent start. My thoughts had to be replaced with other thoughts—totally different thoughts. They had to be replaced with realistic, obtainable dreams; dreams that would come to pass, by my hard and diligent effort.

One of my dreams was to become a published author, so I decided to write this book. This book is just one of many in my heart that I see will come to fruition. I decided to write about the frustrations, hurts, and unnecessary hurdles women face in relationships. I decided to lay it all on the line. This topic is hot and there are so many views on it. Am I saying anything different than anyone else? Maybe yes, or maybe no, but I do know that I am taking the time to say something. I want every woman to read this book and absorb every word. I want to challenge every woman to love herself in truth, and not allow lust to rule her flesh, and ultimately influence her decisions to surrender her body, her perfect gift from God, to a fling—an affair that can only lead to destruction. I desire that every woman will realize that every woman in the limelight is not always fit to be her example. Let God be your example.

> *Your beauty should not come from outward adornment, such as braided hair and the wearing of gold jewelry and fine clothes. Instead, it should be that of your inner self, the unfading beauty of a gentle and quiet spirit, which is of great worth in God's sight. For this is the way the holy women of the past who put their hope in God used to make themselves beautiful (1 Peter 3: 3-5, NIV).*

Let the beautiful queen, Esther, be your example. She beautified herself by preparing herself in character as well as outer beauty for one year to stand before a king—one time—that changed the course of history forever. Let such a woman be your example.

> *Before a girl's turn came—to go in to King Xerxes—she had to complete twelve months of beauty treatments prescribed for the women; six months with oil of myrrh, and six with perfumes and cosmetics. And this is how she would go to the king: anything she wanted was given her to take with her from the harem to the king's palace. In the evening she would go there and in the morning return to another part of the harem to the care of Shaashgaz, the king's eunuch who was in charge of the concubines. She would not return to the king unless he was pleased with her and summoned her by name (Esther 2:12-14, NIV). On the third day*

Esther put on her royal robes and stood in the inner court of the palace, in front of the king's hall. The king was sitting on his royal throne in the hall, facing the entrance. When he saw Queen Esther standing in the court, he was pleased with her and held out to her the gold scepter that was in his hand. So Esther approached and touched the tip of the scepter. Then the king asked, "What is it, Queen Esther? What is your request? Even up to half the kingdom, it will be given you," (Esther 5: 1-3, NIV).

"Esther was a woman of wisdom who knew how to humble herself before her husband. She was willing to be patient and trust that God would deal with her situation. So with her chaste conversation she won the heart of her husband. There is a lot to be said when a king loves a woman so much that he would be willing to give her half his kingdom."

It is God's perfect will for all of mankind to be loved and to give love. However, He does not want His most perfect gift to be distorted and to bring hurt and defeat to people's lives. This was never His intent, yet, so many have experienced only the negativity and pitfalls of relationships. Many people have never experienced the joy and splendor that permeates the relationships for which real, true love was intended.

Can you stand to be alone? Of course you can if you have a purpose and begin to spend time fulfilling your purpose. Begin to go inside of yourself to explore the untapped gifts and talents you possess. Begin to allow those gifts and talents to develop so that they may be shared with the world. Remember, I stated that you spend more time with yourself than with anyone else. Get to really know you, and begin to love you, and watch that self-love begin to draw that special someone to you. Take this time to appreciate those people that God has already placed in your life. Take this time to get to know those who genuinely love you. Stop pushing them away, as we often do. And, as the old Isley Brothers' song says, *Love the One You're With.* Love yourself, love others; and before long, you will find yourself strolling through the park with your handsome beau, or taking your walk down that aisle. You will be the envy of all your friends (smile).

"I discovered that being alone was a good thing and I was okay with it. That was the best time to work on some short term and long term goals, and working on myself would be the perfect solution to fill the void in my life. Begin to go inside of yourself to explore the untapped gifts and talents you possess."

Chapter 3
Questions To Consider

1. Do you have strong feelings of despair because you feel alone and lonely? Are you suffering from depression?

   Write down five activities that you would like to get involved in(i.e. going to the spa, etc.).
   a.
   b.
   c.
   d.
   e.

2. Reflect on your daily activities and then ask yourself what you do to keep yourself busy so that you won't feel lonely. If you don't do anything, consider adding the activities listed in number two to your life to fill the void.

3. Is your loneliness or 'alone feeling' due to a lack of spirituality? Do you feel that you are searching and in need of developing a closer relationship with God?

4. If you answered yes to question four, please recite the following prayer aloud.

"Father,
I am feeling lonely and alone. I know that
it is not your will that I feel this way.
I long to have that emptiness filled
and I've tried filling it with things that
couldn't fulfill me. Please come into
my life and reveal your love to me
in a special way.
I need you to fill that void in my
life and I expect you to do it.
Thank you Father.
In Jesus name,
Amen."

Chapter Four

Looking Content

Have you ever met a woman who appeared to be so very happy with herself and her life that you were drawn just to meet her and find out the secret of her contentment? Well, this, surprisingly, had happened to me. I was the one being admired and I did not realize that this aura was emanating from within me. It happened when I could stand to be alone.

As mentioned earlier, I was an Adult Education teacher and I had the pleasure of teaching some very special people. I had come to cherish and respect many of them. Because I was aspiring to be a motivational speaker/empowerment trainer, I tried hard to convey a certain image and attitude to my students. For many of them, I was the most positive person in their lives. So evidently my efforts had not been in vain. A few of my students told me that I carried myself like I was content, and I even get that response, presently. Well, I asked them what they meant. They indicated that I carried myself like I was married, or at least, in a loving relationship. They equated contentment with being in a positive relationship. I found that to be surprisingly interesting.

I would not tell anyone that you must be married or in a good relationship to be, or look, content. But looking like we are content and happy with life should be our goal. No one has arrived in perfecting every area of his or her lives, so striving to work at it should be a daily task.

What I believe my students saw was a look of hopeful anticipation of happiness and the realization that all women should anticipate being found by that ideal man. The gleam in my eye was the hope for change, the pep in my step was the faith I held, and the positive attitude I displayed was the assurance that someday my prayers would be answered—for a soul mate that would efficiently complement me.

Being content is certainly something we all need to work towards, because frustration would very easily step in the way if we were not careful. Frustration can cause us all to do some crazy things, which we often greatly regret.

I recall a time when I managed a shelter for homeless women and children. It was a dream job because I was touching people's lives and it was the first time I was ever responsible for managing anything of that magnitude. I managed eight to ten staff members and was responsible for the lives and welfare of about thirty women and children.

Everything was running smoothly until a jealous staff person informed the director that I was working for both the Board of Education and the shelter. The director knew this when he hired me as the shelter manager. I taught GED/ABE in the morning and around 3:30 pm, I started working for the shelter as a counselor. This went on for a few months until school was out for the summer. I believed that the pastor was very impressed with me and he watched how I interacted with the residents of the shelter. I got along fairly well with the ladies and I thought the staff liked me too.

The pastor came to me one day and asked me if I would like to be the shelter manager. He told me he liked how I handled the residents and he trusted me. Now there was a staff person who felt that she should have gotten the position. She was jealous but she hid it very well. She did everything in her power to sabotage my efforts. Every mistake I made got back to the pastor and she would deliberately set me up to fail because she knew I was still learning my position. Because I trusted her, I took her advice on certain issues. Many of the decisions were not right

She was real chummy with the pastor's wife, who never even took the time to come over to meet me. I felt she was very immature for a pastor's wife. She was an ex-drug addict and it was quite evident that she had a lot of growing up to do. Oh, I forgot to mention that this staff person was also an ex-resident of the shelter and she felt that she should have been the manager. In fact I mentioned that to the pastor and he told me that he did not trust her.

I worked there for little or nothing, but I did a lot of good things at the shelter and I made a great friend who I still fellowship with to this day. I began to become overwhelmed because I was always on call. The Pastor did not want to have anything to do with the shelter, and when something went wrong they, the shelter staff, were supposed to call me. I had a life too, but evidently he did not think so. If something went wrong or if there arose a situation that they were unfamiliar with, they would call me, and if I was not available, they would call him. This would make him so angry. Then it had gotten to the point that they would call him just because it would cause him to angrily talk to me any old kind of way. I would politely remind him that he was able to take two major trips because of my being over the shelter and I told him that he never gave me a cell phone or a pager so that anyone could reach me when I was not working.

Things just went from bad to worse and he eventually asked me to leave. He stated that someone came to him and said that it was not fair that I was collecting two paychecks. I left the shelter position and I returned to solely teaching.

Now, it is difficult to explain all the emotions that were playing around inside me, but I can say frustration was definitely at the top of the list. I also felt betrayed and rejected. That time had to be one of the loneliest times in my life, because I felt everyone in the building was against me. I had to continue working there because my teaching assignment was in the shelter. I did not know who was for me or who was against me.

I know for a fact that when your mind is not at peace, you find yourself doing incredibly foolish things. I definitely was not in the right frame of mind when I allowed myself to fall for a guy who lived in the men's shelter. In fact, the men's shelter was the original shelter before they opened the women's shelter, which was founded about two years later. Now, getting back to this fellow that I met. Upon first impression, he was truly a beautiful person. He was down on his luck at the time, and my being quite vulnerable; fell for his hard luck story. I latter found out that he was one of the men with whom I should not have been involved with, ever.

My mother's famous saying is, 'Loneliness makes strange friends and strange bedfellows.' I was about to play right into the hands of loneliness. What possessed me to take up time with a man who did not have anything going for him but a pleasant smile and personality? Was I that miserable? This man was the twentieth century Dr. Jekyll and Mr. Hyde. This man was a psycho. He had the worst temper, was insecure to the third degree, and had a triple addiction—drugs, alcohol, and gambling.

I moved this guy into my home hoping to help him get on his feet. He was very generous and an extremely hard worker. He was very handy around the house. I liked this guy too. Even though he was from a shelter, I thought he would be different from the other guys. We could talk about anything and we always laughed. He also had the most beautiful smile. We spent a lot of time at the park (Belle Isle) just holding hands and making plans for the future. I even took this man to my church. At the time, I was attending a church in Plymouth, Michigan. Everything was going fine, I thought. We had even talked about getting married. Then it happened. Will the real psycho please stand up? I recall we were in the basement one day. He was working on a cleaning project, and I asked him a question about something he was doing that I did not agree with. He went off on me. I had never seen this side of him. He hollered at me at the top of his lungs. I stood there just looking at him. This was the beginning of a down hill relationship. From that moment on, there was not too much I could say to him without him wanting to argue with me and try to intimidate me by hollering. This man had at least three different personalities. I did not know what bag he was coming out of most of the time.

Now I am about to reveal something to you that I am not proud of but I told you I was going to keep it real. One day we had an argument in my kitchen and he thought that he would try and intimidate me by getting up in my face. Now, any man should know that you do not get up in a woman's face, especially a black woman. Well, you can kind of guess what happened next. No? Well, let me satisfy your curiosity. I did the unthinkable; I bit him on his nose. I tried to bite his nose off. Yes, that is right and there is still a scar there today unless he had plastic surgery. I am not a violent person. So this was my clue to get away from this man before I badly and fatally hurt him or he hurt me.

My God! What had I gotten myself into? These were the thoughts that ran through my head as I planned to get this loser out of my life. When I got rid of him, there was not a day that did not go by that I did not thank God for bringing me out of this situation. I was so ashamed that I allowed myself to stoop that low, and I begged God for His forgiveness. I had lost my contentment. I became vulnerable. I allowed the situation at the shelter to cloud my judgment. This situation located me. I realized that staying content is a mindset, and it should not change from situation to situation. Life is always going to have its challenges but we have to remain constant in our way of thinking. I fell again because I did not keep my guard up. I went to that familiar way out which was destructive. I sabotaged myself.

When I started working at the shelter, I thought I was happy and content with my life. I thought I was satisfied with my life. I had just bought a new home that October, 1994 and a new car that November. I was riding high, but evidently there was a doorway that was not guarded, and I fell prey to that temptation of having the wrong person fill the void and act as my savior. I lost my focus and I took my eyes off of God and looked at man. I opened the door for that situation to over take me and it almost did.

Hard times and disappointments are going to come. This is inevitable, but do not allow yourselves to get caught in a snare. Stay positive and surround yourselves with positive people. Do not be tempted to be a Lone Ranger. Allow others to become a part of your contentment process. That is what family and close friends are for. People who are close to you become an umbrella for our lives and can often shield us from making unhealthy choices when we are in a slumber. Contentment is based on one's frame of mind. It comes from making a choice to be that way.

For as he thinketh in his heart, so is he
(Proverbs 23:7, KJV).

When I reflect back on my student who thought I was content, I realized that there was power in my aura. There was a sense of tranquility and peace that I wanted to obtain and maintain. You are invincible when you are content. Bad intentions cannot filter in when that shield of contentment is up. This is why we are instructed to be content and be anxious for nothing. Anxiousness destroys our chemical balance that is so necessary for the human body to maintain good health and a long life. When that balance is tampered with, all kinds of doorways are opened that can also introduce sickness and disease. Trust me, I know first hand and I'll tell you about it in my next book, THIS IS A COMMA IN YOUR LIFE, NOT A PERIOD.

Do not be anxious about anything, but in
everything, by prayer and petition, with thanksgiving,
present your requests to God (Philippians 4: 6, NIV).

Make the decision to be content. It is a very peaceful and pleasant place to be. It is the place where the next level of your life can begin, because you are in a state of gratefulness. Good things happen to people who can appreciate and recognize the blessings they already have. It builds a healthy character and allows us to reap the benefits of obtaining a wholesome lifestyle. When you are content, you don't have to compromise and you don't have to worry about getting into a snare that can affect you for the rest of your life. Be encouraged and know with all of your heart—All is well!

"The gleam in my eye was the hope for change, the pep in my step was the faith I held, and the positive attitude I displayed was the assurance that someday my prayers (would be answered) for a soul mate that would efficiently complement me."

Chapter 4
Questions To Consider

1. Are you anxious to have a man in your life? If you answered "yes", slow down and begin appreciating the time that you spend with yourself and others.

2. In waiting for that person you long to be with, you should be working on being content. Allow me to offer you some suggestions:

   a. Daily pray the prayer you just read in chapter 3.
   b. Daily adorn yourself—make it your business to always look your best(i.e. hair, makeup, colors, fashion).
   c. Surround yourself with people who are in healthy, nurturing relationships.
   d. Get a hobby and/or find activities that you enjoy doing.
   e. Write down the characteristics you would like to present to your mate and work on them.

CHAPTER FIVE

The Woman in the Mirror

One of my favorite songs that famed entertainer Michael Jackson recorded was *Man in the Mirror*. This song dealt with self-examination of one's character, and it is something that I would dare to say many people do not do. Let's be honest. How many of you can truly say that you work on developing your character like you work on losing weight, getting a good paying job or just impressing people any way that you can?

Ladies, if we are going to be the best we can be, then we are going to have to use that bathroom mirror for more than just applying our make-up and adorning the outside. We must begin working on adorning the inside person which is our character and personality.

As I reflect on how the world places celebrities on a pedestal, it saddens me that they do not reflect the image of always being a positive role model. Many of their lifestyles leave much to be desired. I understand that they are human and subject to error, but many of them do not care about what is right or wrong. They just do their thing no matter what anyone says or what the consequences might be.

I recall one year at the Grammy awards, one of the sultriest singers in the music industry came on stage practically naked.

Now, you raise your eyebrows and say to yourselves, "That is probably half the singers who receive an award or do the presentations" Well, this one came from the home of a preacher. I am not trying to pick on her because she is the preacher's kid. I have singled her out because she was taught to fear God and respect and keep his commandments; at least this was what she confessed. I suppose she does not realize that young women admire her and they look to her to set an example for them. If I were to confront her and ask her why she dresses like that, she would probably curse me out and tell me to mind my own business; but not before reminding me that she is a great singer, and she is giving the public and her fans what they want. She and so many others would rather be labeled as being one of the sexiest women in the world than be labeled as the most respected and admired for her wholesomeness and uncompromising behavior as a lady. No, that image does not win Grammy awards.

I am sure that many people would not see anything wrong with a woman coming on stage practically naked. I am sure that most of those people are not even aware that this behavior depicts a lack of character and moral standards. It is nothing to see and hear of the immorality that is displayed today. In fact, if you happen to be a watcher of sitcoms, you will see homosexuality being glamorized; women every other week changing boyfriends and women acting desperate by running after men who do not want them. But I am sure that all of these people would be insulted if they were to be challenged and told that they played roles that lacked character and set a poor example for our very impressionable children and young adults.

It is time out for this kind of behavior to continue to depict what should be the norm. When will we get to the place when we begin to realize that something is wrong with our reasoning and behavior? Something is desperately wrong when an actress gets an Oscar because she was displayed on the big screen enjoying oral sex. And yet no one thought enough of her performance when she played the heart felt role of a drug addict who lost her baby to the system and tried desperately to get him back. What is this world coming to?

Now, earlier I mentioned working on both character and personality. I do not want you to get them mixed up. Believe it or not, character and personality are two separate entities. One deals with the inner characteristics and the other deals with the outer self. But the character very much shapes and molds our personalities based on our experiences and attitudes that have developed through how we interpreted our experiences.

Let me expound on this. A person can have a very pleasant personality (your outer quality that is seen), but have hidden agendas such as maliciousness and jealousy (character traits that are inner qualities). We all know people with these qualities who act very nice and are a lot of fun, but do not get too close because their venom might kill you. Like snakes, they can be packaged in a variety of beautiful colors, but their nature is to entrap their victims and destroy them. Sister to sister, some of us can be a trip. We know that we need to work on some areas of our character so that we will not always belong to the 'Love 'em and leave 'em' club. That is the club where the man is the person leaving. Let's be for real about it, some of us need a major attitude adjustment. We are not always pleasant and desirable because of some our apparent character flaws which would be a turn-off to any normal, red-blooded male.

Now, I am not trying to come down on sisters because I realize we have experienced a lot of disappointments and we have taken on a lot of burdens that have left many of us very resentful and bitter. Too often, we enter into relationships with our guard up, and this is a wise thing to do, but our lack of trust is also very prevalent. We are all guilty of allowing past mishaps to threaten our future love connections. Ladies, this can be a very ugly situation if allowed to get out of hand. With the lack of trust come her big sisters jealousy, envy and strife. Again, these all deal with character and personality. There are many other areas that I could discuss, but I do not want to get that deep. This is not a book of psychology that deals with human behavior. I am sure you get my drift.

Let's continue to examine ourselves daily. Always be your best critic. Note that I did not say worst critic. Self-criticism should not be destructive. Looking at the woman in the mirror will help us maintain a positive outlook toward others and ourselves. We want to strive to be the best person we can be. It is not okay to act ugly and expect others to accept you that way. My mom always told me as a child, growing up, that 'pretty is as pretty does.'

I recall several years ago, I welcomed a woman (into my home) that fell on hard times. One of the brothers of my former church asked me to allow her to move in. I did allow her to move in and I tried to make her feel as comfortable as possible. At first we got along beautifully and everything was going fine. Then suddenly the real she-devil surfaced and she began to turn on me. She accused me of stealing her clothes when in fact she left them in the trunk of my car accidentally when she moved in. She would deliberately pick arguments with me and the straw that broke the camel's back was when she cooked a meal and messed up the stove when the food boiled over on several isles. I insisted that she clean it up and I asked her to move out also. She refused to clean the stove. So I did not let her take her clothes (that was definitely a mistake) and she flagged down the police and brought them to my home and told them that I kicked her out and refused to let her get her clothes. The police immediately noticed that something was desperately wrong with her, and encouraged me to allow her to take her clothes out of my home, and be rid of her forever. Well, that was the last time I saw her and I realized that her nice personality had me fooled but the real person finally had to show herself. You know what they say, "You never know a person until you live with them."

This woman had some unresolved issues she never dealt with. So she covered them up instead of exposing them so that they could be disposed of. She is like thousands of others who go through life never working on being a better person.

Unfortunately, we live in a society where the emphasis is placed on achievements, material possessions, and status not character. We will give a graduation party to someone who completed a four-year degree program but how many people are honored for having integrity? Hey, I just wanted to put something on your mind.

There is nothing more beautiful than a woman who is in control of herself and knows what and when certain emotions and actions are truly appropriate to display. Temperance is the key to beauty and it is just one beautiful characteristic of the human spirit. There are eight more. The word of God calls this group the fruit of the Spirit, which is something that you cannot earn, nor is it freely given.

> *But the fruit of the Spirit is love, joy, peace,*
> *Long-suffering, gentleness, goodness, faith,*
> *meekness and temperance*
> *(Galatians 5:22, KJV).*

It is the part of the human spirit and character that must be developed. If you know there are areas in your life and character that are not appealing, take the time, especially if you are not in a relationship right now, to work on YOU. Remember, 'Pretty is as pretty does,' and also know this: just like you want him to be at his best, he deserves the same from you.

"Self-criticism should not be destructive. Looking at the woman in the mirror will help us maintain a positive outlook toward others and ourselves."

Chapter 5
Questions To Consider

1. It is very important to work on inner beauty before we work on the outer beauty. Unfortunately, we live in a society that doesn't place a lot of emphasis on character. I believe that in order to attract that ideal person, you have to work on being the best that you can be. Remember, "Pretty is as pretty does." Identify at least three character flaws you know you must work on.

2. Do you believe that these character flaws can hinder you from getting or keeping your mate?

3. Are you a woman who feels that outer adornment is all a woman needs to attract a man? If you strongly feel this way, where did this come from?

4. Do this exercise—tell one friend about a character flaw you want to work on and ask him or her to help you work on it. Consciously work on changing this for fourteen days and after the fourteenth day asks your friend if he or she has noticed a change in you in that area. Work on it until that flaw is gone. Success to you!

C H A P T E R S I X

Preparation Is Not Lost Time

66 "P*reparation is not lost time',* was the message I heard
from the singles minister at one of my former
churches. This was around eighteen years ago
when I attended Jubilee Christian Church. I never forgot those
words that Minister Isha Williams expressed at a singles meeting
and they stuck with me all these years.

Preparing seems to be how I have spent the past eighteen
years of my life. Getting ready for the ministry and that life-long
companion that God's getting ready to manifest into my life. I
am waiting with anticipation. But, in the meantime, I must get
busy working on those areas of my life that need bettering. I
needed to work on those flaws in my character and start to further
develop the gifts and talents God placed inside of me: making
use of the valuable time that I have by getting my temple (body)
together, losing weight and working on my image; getting my
house together by improving its inner and outer appearance,
and developing strong relationships with people God placed
in my life.

One of the areas I am working on now is getting the business/
ministry (off the ground) that God has given me to do. I have
started networking and getting the foundation of the ministry I
have laid. I am writing books like this one, along with textbooks

and tapes for my workshops and seminars. This is my DREAM. Being a motivational speaker and empowerment trainer has been a long-time dream, but I had to complete other tasks first before actually stepping out into this calling. I label my dream as 'a calling' because I believe that God divinely ordained this wondrous task. He placed this desire in my heart; therefore, I am assured that He will equip me to do it. But first things first, I had worked diligently at improving myself before I could effectively minister to others about improving themselves.

I would encourage anyone who desired a helpmate to first work on those personal areas that can be accomplished without a mate: loose the excess weight, go after the degree you have always wanted, start that ministry or business you have in your heart; perfect your image, start reading empowerment books written by both Christian and secular authors; travel and see the world, get involved in your community by doing volunteer work, or become a mentor. This list can go on and on.

It took some time for me to really get this revelation because I was stuck on feeling sorry for myself. Things were not going the way I thought they should be going. I found myself battling with depression and feeling anxious all of the time. I was not settled in my spirit and hopelessness entered in. I wanted to be married and nothing or no one could make me feel any differently. I am supposed to be married and this part of my life should be fulfilled by now. I really believed that God did not want me to be married because I was still reaping what I sowed from all the past mistakes I had made. I walked with condemnation as my constant companion. I did not feel worthy.

I supposed that making it happen could have been an option but I was just tired of the games. I began to reflect on my past relationships and I knew that I had no regrets for not being with any of those men. Then suddenly, a wonderful feeling came over me and I realized that there was much hope. That right guy was still out there and there was no mess in my life, therefore there was much room and opportunity for me to meet him. When I began to look at the situation differently, I felt happy and peaceful. Although there are no prospects for marriage yet, I am okay with that. I feel at peace and I like having this time to get myself together. I hope whoever he is, he too, is working on himself. I would like to think so.

Now I spend my days working on getting myself together. I am planning fundraisers, and I am even teaching a self-esteem class at my church. I am also working on losing the excess weight—I am very determined this time. I was recently ordained and licensed as an Elder and Evangelist. I also became a part of a very prominent Christian organization who licensed me to minister in a greater capacity. There will be no distractions and no time limit either. I am also working on my books and other mini projects, but above all, I am working on getting closer to God. I do love Him and I desire to get to know Him better and be used mightily by Him.

This time alone can actually be the best time of your life, because you can spend this time getting to know one of the most precious of God's creations—YOU. Preparation is not lost time! Preparation is the first step toward being fulfilled in this life. Time is going to become your best friend, you will see.

"Preparation is not lost time . . . loose the excess weight, go after the degree you have always wanted, start that ministry or business you have in your heart;, perfect your image, start reading empowerment books written by both Christian and secular authors, travel and see the world, get involved in your community by doing volunteer work, or become a mentor."

Chapter 6
Questions To Consider

1. What are you doing to prepare for your mate?—i.e. (lose weight).

2. Have you asked God to show you the areas you need to work on to get ready to receive what he has for you?

3. Make God a major participant in your preparatory process. By doing this, you will sense that this process is not solely yours to do and there is another responsible partner that is greatly concerned about your progress.

CHAPTER SEVEN

You've Got To Be the One To Get the One

We often hear the expression, 'opposites attract', and that is fine if you are talking about magnets. But complete opposite couples are bound to end up broken-hearted, because they are going to soon find out that they have little or nothing in common.

I am really disheartened when I think of the many couples who do not make it because they did not take the time to access whether or not they were going to be spiritually, morally, and economically compatible. This was a trend that I witnessed more with males than with females, but of course, it is true for us, also.

I want to elaborate on some things. As I wrote in earlier chapters, I was an adult education teacher; and of course, I had male students. Sometimes Cupid shoots his arrow to try to make a love connection. These were men who did not possess a high school diploma, used deplorable English, and were either under or unemployed. They were attracted to me. But what did we have in common? What could they bring to the table? I am not solely speaking of material possessions. Could we have possessed the same values? Did we have the same or similar goals? Could we have held an intelligent conversation? Were we spiritually compatible? I am not trying to imply that we must be on the same spiritual level, but I do believe that being equally yoked is very important in making a relationship work.

Although I was guilty of getting involved with one of my male students, I realized that my attraction was to his physical appearance. Physical attraction is often the determining factor for couples coming together, and that is so unfortunate. We must learn to look beyond the physical, and scrutinize the whole situation and background of the person we are considering getting involved with. I got caught up with this man because he fit the profile of my ideal man from a physical perspective, and that entangled me as it does so many women. The only thing on my mind was being intimate with him because he was so attractive to me. I was also attractive to him, so that made being good even harder. My every thought was about him, and I felt those butterflies in my stomach when he was near me. I truly could not help myself. I knew I did not need to be with this man because beyond being intimate, there was no future. I had to wake up and smell the coffee. It saddened me to know that here was a man I was falling in love with, but we did not have a real chance at a future because we had nothing in common outside of the bedroom. In addition to his lack of education, he was still involved with his ex. The drama was too great for me to play a part in. The web that he was creating could have been deadly if I did not let it go in time. He was not a violent person, but he was very argumentative and had to have the last word. I am a peacemaker, and do not enjoy being in such a challenging position just to have someone in my life.

I wish that people would take the time and evaluate the situation before they just jump into it. All is not fair in love and war. True love is the key to happiness, and when we allow ourselves to get involved with just the physical part of a person, we loose. Open up your eyes and see the total package; it is okay if you do not like what you see. Move on. Do not become entangled because it looks and feels good to you; get involved because it is good to you and for you.

If we want to attract a certain type of person, we should have similar values and goals in life. We should have something to contribute to enhance the other person's life. Just as you may think the other person is special, you must be special too. They want God's best just as you do.

"Physical attraction is often the determining factor for couples coming together, and that is so unfortunate."

A few years ago, I dated a guy who really had it going, or so I thought; and he told me something very profound. It hurt me, but it gave me something to think about. I told him how much I thought he added to my life, and I was learning so much from him. Well, he in turn told me that he was not learning anything from me, and I was not really contributing anything to his life. WOW! Talking about a rude awakening. I soon discovered later that he was very arrogant and harsh. Although it hurt me when he said that, and I now know what motivated that statement, that is true for many people involved in relationships. It is dead because there is no spiritual, mental, or emotional stimulation. This is very much needed if the relationship is to have any substance. These components give the relationship it's staying power; believe it or not.

Many articles have been written on professional women dating and marrying blue-collar workers, and the bliss that comes from that union. These relationships worked because there were other strong factors they both had in common. It could be that they were spiritually compatible. Maybe they had the same values about family and education, or maybe they both had similar long-term goals. These are just a few examples of areas that couples with different levels of education and professions may have in common. These commonalities, in turn, become the glue that binds them. So you see, compatibility is not just based on education and economic status, although it does help, but it is based on inner qualities. You have got to be one to get one. As mentioned in the chapter, *Preparation Is Not Lost Time*, begin to access what you really want out of a relationship; whether it is a platonic or romantic union. You want to attract someone who's going in the same direction.

Do two walk together unless they have agreed to do
so? (Amos 3:3, NIV)

I do not know about you, but I want to be in a relationship for life, and I want to enjoy it. If I have to wait a little while longer, then so be it. I am tired of being a statistic and a candidate to be a guest on some of those talk shows. I am in no hurry to make another mistake or ruin my chances of meeting 'Mr. Right'. I am going to make sure that that ideal man is not a fantasy that I got out of Gentleman's Quarterly magazine, and more importantly, I am going to make sure that I am that special woman for him. Make a decision to make this your goal too.

"Many articles have been written on professional women dating and marrying blue-collar workers, and the bliss that comes from that union. These relationships work because there were other strong factors they both had in common. These commonalities, in turn, become the glue that binds them."

Chapter 7
Questions To Consider

1. How often do we find ourselves mentally making a list of the characteristics we want to see in our dream guy or girl? Then when we meet someone, that mental pictures pops up and we find ourselves comparing them to that mental image. This mental imagery is totally unfair, especially if you don't measure up to that which you are expecting from someone else. Identify on a piece of paper the characteristics you are looking for in your mate.

2. Identify on that same piece of paper the characteristics and qualities you have to bring into the relationship.

3. Are your prerequisites realistic?

4. Re-examine your expectations and ask yourself, should they be lowered or brought up a notch or two?

5. Look at the person in the mirror—Do you possess the qualities you want your mate to possess?

Yesterday Is Dead, Today Is Born

O ne of life's greatest challenges is letting go of the past. Even if we do not spend hours crying about past hurts, we somehow allow those past hurts to influence our attitude and behavior towards present events. No matter what our confessions might be, there are still some emotional ghosts that continue to haunt us, and they always surface when we are about to enter into a new relationship. Those small issues somehow become magnified to the tenth degree, and we cannot get past it or around it.

Falling in love can be a very uncomfortable feeling, and, of course, we should put up our guard. That 'love feeling' is life's greatest mystery, yet it is the most sure thing that exists in this life. Although our past hurts may resurface, we owe it to ourselves to allow the heart an opportunity to love again.

I can travel back down memory lane and think about all my past hurts and great disappointments. If I dwell on them long enough, it would probably make me extremely depressed. Today, it is about laughter and joy, and the fresh breeze of the wind across my face on a sunny spring day. I do not want to be consumed by the hurts of my past. I want to love and be loved.

Sometimes I can feel the passion swelling up inside, just ready to explode. It hurts just having to hold my love inside, knowing that there is someone out there whose life I could make just a little sweeter by having him in my presence, to receive the affection I am longing to give him. But if I hold on to the past, the present becomes smothering, and the future suddenly seems to disappear.

When I pray, I often remind God that He did not intend for man to be alone, and there is a lonely man out there somewhere, longing to meet me. If I allowed my past hurts to dictate to me, I would not have even prayed that prayer. I believe that I have gotten over a great deal of the hurts, but I am sure there is some residue of pain left. I work through the pain by encouraging other women and through writing this book. As my fingers stroke each key to formulate the words, my healing is taking place. The words are flowing so fluently in my head as I type them.

Trust me when I tell you, I paid a price for this restoration. I was afflicted with cancer because I allowed the bitterness to settle in my body, and the hatred that I felt for some of those men turned to cancerous tumors. You see, we do not realize that the opposite of love, which is hate, can kill us; as well as the presence of love can heal us. I had to learn the hard way, to let go of the past. It is not easy when there are so many things from your past that are somehow still in your present, staring at you, haunting you, forever reminding you of its deeds.

My hell began when I married my ex-husband on March 21, 1979. I was twenty-one years old, and I married a young man from Lagos, Nigeria while attending college at the University of Detroit. He was the most controlling and manipulative man I had ever met, yet, his experiences intrigued me. There was never a dull moment with him. I was not in love with him, but I loved him, and I could not imagine my life without him; yet, I did not want to be married to him. This man had a hold on me that I could not explain to you, even if you paid me a million dollars to do it.

"When I pray, I often remind God that he did not intend for man to be alone and that there is a lonely man out there somewhere longing to meet me."

Before we were married, we would sit in his dorm room for hours and talk. I would travel to different countries in my mind as he told me of his adventures. By the time he was twenty years old, he had already traveled halfway around the world. He was educated in England and his English was impeccable. He exposed me to a world that I would have only read about. I would sit and listen to him in awe of all the wonderful things he experienced. I could not understand why this well—traveled man would want a young inexperienced woman from the ghettos of Detroit.

I knew that I should not have ever married him. We were both immature and selfish and I came out of a broken home raised by a single mother. So I did not know how to hang in there when things got rough. I literally cried and begged God to let me divorce him. He was a faithful husband and provided for his family on a minimum wage salary. He was brilliant, but because he was not a citizen of this country, he was unable to get a good—paying job. We suffered greatly and we did not get along because of it. We had the responsibility of a baby and it was very hard on his ego not being able to provide for us in the fashion in which he thought we deserved. We were divorced three years later and my journey as a single mother began. It was a hell that I was not prepared for at all. He left the U.S and went back to his country where he has resided ever since.

I lived with many regrets and I wished that I could turn back the hands of time, but it is okay now. I look forward to the future and I realize that those other men were just fill ins. If I had not gone through those things there would not be a book to write and I could not impact anyone's life the way I have. I went through it, I came through it, and now I am going to share with others the lessons that I learned, and I hope that these lessons will stop many of you from making the same mistakes.

We all make mistakes. We all have been victims, and we have made someone else the victim. So what are we going to do about it? Part of being forgiven for one's mistakes involve forgiving one's self. Do not allow others to continue to throw past mistakes in your face, or remind you of past disappointments. Rise above that, begin to rejoice and know that the future definitely holds good things for you. The only people that have permission to live in the past are the dead, because they are literally stuck there. Even Jesus has a remedy for letting go of the past. He said,

"Let the dead bury the dead" (Matthew 8: 22, KJV).

In other words, it is over for them, and if you want to spend time grieving about how it was or how it might have been, you will never reach your future hopes and dreams that have been written in your book of life. It will forever be a never-ending story about your past.

"The only people that have permission to live in the past are the dead, because they are literally stuck there."

Chapter 8
Questions To Consider

1. Letting go of the past is sometimes one of our greatest challenges. Our past mistakes have been known to haunt us and keep us trapped in an abyss of hopelessness, but it's time to look forward to the future and take an active role in it. Let's begin by denouncing negative feelings and thoughts we may have about ourselves. Begin to look inward for the strength, courage, and direction we need to capture and live happily in the future. Write down past mistakes that have been haunting you and hindering you from going forward.

2. If these mistakes revolve around a man or woman, openly admit your part and forgive yourself. Openly admit their part and forgive them.

3. If you are struggling with unforgiveness, let me give you a revelation. Forgiveness is for you. It releases you from a great spiritual trap that can lead to sickness and disease, such as depression and cancer. Allow me to walk you through an exercise that will assist you in this plight. Write down the names of the people you are having difficulty forgiving.

Repeat this affirmation:

*I forgive (say the name of the person)
by faith and I choose to love them.
My love is greater than the hurt and pain
they inflicted on me and I release them.
I'm making a conscious decision to
go forward in my life and I'm not
taking these past relationships with me.*

Note: You can also say this in the form of a prayer
by adding *"Father"* or *"Lord"* and ending the
affirmation with *"Amen."*

Tear and throw away the piece of paper,
smile, and get on with your life.

Chapter Nine

It Is Your Time

Well, we have made our mistakes and we have done our apologies. Who do we owe now? How long must we carry the burden of our past mishaps? When do we begin to shut out the people who continue to point the finger and throw the stones? We cannot continue to waddle in the mess. It is time for a change. It is time for a second chance, a third chance, a fourth chance. However many chances it takes, it is time. It is your time.

As we travel down that new road let's begin to keep in mind that we have not been where we are going, and we do not want to revisit where we have been. The time capsule is full and there is only enough room for you in it. Not your friends, not your family, not your pastor, nor old boyfriends; no one but you. This is your journey: a journey of new beginnings, a journey of hope, and a journey full of joy. So sit back, buckle your seat belt and enjoy the ride.

These are the words I had to start believing and allowing to enter my spirit after my ordeal with my ex-friend (fiancé) Lee. I had to tell myself that now it is time for ME! After I carried the frustration, heartache and guilt around for so long, I knew that continuing to go on like that would be very destructive. It was time to shift gears and regroup. It had to be all about

Tunishai, and yes, some people may not understand my new found conviction, but it did not change the fact that it had to be done.

I had to make a new list of short-term goals that I wanted to accomplish by the end of 1999 and the year of 2000. I started working on improving my prayer life, and became determined that His voice was the only voice I would seek for guidance. I did not feel like being mislead anymore by people with oh—so—good intentions that were leading me straight into the devil's pit. It was time to start trusting my heart, my spirit, and me. I placed too much trust in man and not enough in God and myself. If you were to ask me what was the lesson learned from this experience, I would have to say, to trust the inner voice in me, not to always go with popular opinion, and not to be afraid anymore of being alone. In essence, I was never left alone, because my best buddy, Jesus, was always and will always be present with me.

> " . . . God has said, 'never will I leave you; never will I forsake you'" (Hebrews 13: 5b, NIV).

It was the year 2003 and I was still striving to reach my goals and God had a way of redirecting them. I started teaching a self-esteem class at my church, Immanuel House of Prayer, and I really enjoyed it. I believed that the women in attendance were enjoying it too. I went to my pastor with a proposal to start a women's ministry there under the ministry that God has given me, Your Own Uniqueness. It did not happen the way I believed God gave it to me, but maybe it would end up that way. We have to trust that He knows what is best for us and when He tells us something, we need to believe. If it kept me busy and I could be a blessing to other women, then I would be okay. I was sure that eventually I will be operating full time in the ministry God gave me in the near future.

I am alone but I am not lonely. I am anticipating being found but I am not looking. I am working on staying busy and productive. I stay out of trouble when I am busy and less likely to entertain negative thoughts. It is not my job to look. I am happy that that burden has not been placed on the woman. All we have to do is stay busy and concentrate on the task before us, and that is obtaining God's best. Now if you feel like you can relate to what I am saying, I say, bravo! Be honest with yourselves and allow the healing to begin by spending time with the most important, significant and unique person God made—YOU! Truly let go of the past and if necessary, the people who try to keep you bound to the past. Make a list of goals and dreams that you have and get busy working on them.

So you made some mistakes. Who has not? There are glass houses out there with many cracks in them, but yours does not have to be one of them. Begin to rebuild and re-love yourself. Cherish these new beginnings and the lessons learned from your past. But do not store them in your memory. Let it go and remember IT IS YOUR TIME. The time capsule is only large enough for one person, and that person is beautiful you.

"I am alone but I am not lonely. I am anticipating being found but I am not looking."

Chapter 9
Questions To Consider

1. Well, you have identified what you want in a man or woman. You know what you need to do to change and you've stepped out of the past into forgiveness and healing. Now it's time to execute a game plan for greatness. Begin to see yourself as the most wonderful person in the universe and desiring to share yourself with the world. Begin working on those things you have always desired to do(i.e. lose weight, start a business, go back to school, write a book, etc.). Remember it's your time. Utilize it to the hilt. Don't waste the greatest commodity God has given you. Write down your goals—realistic ones and short term, and actively and faithfully start working on them.

2. Tell a good friend what you are doing. This will help with accountability. If someone else knows you are trying to accomplish something, (i.e. losing weight, etc.) you will be less likely to cheat.

Chapter Ten

I Miss the Hugs
But Not the Hurts

I imagine you are wondering to yourself where did she come up with such a catchy title for this book? Well, like everything I come up with, it was inspired. Someone I cared very much for inspired it. I thought he was the one for me and I hoped that we could really have a wonderful relationship. Well, all I got was a fast roller coaster ride and I did not enjoy it at all. I started seeing this man on my job at Harris school. Yes, I know what you are thinking to yourselves right now. Harris has a lot of history for me.

I met John; I will call him that. When I made up my mind that I was going to stop looking and just start to relax a little, John came along. He was one of my co-workers and he really had it all together, I thought. We had been working in the same building for about six months before we noticed each other or shall I say when I noticed him. The day he acknowledged me was a day that I was feeling very good about myself. I had a brand new hair-do (braids), a beautiful purple, knit two—piece that my mother gave me, and my make-up was on just right. I was a teacher and he was a computer technician. He worked in another part of the building, but I had to pass by his workstation daily to make copies.

This particular day, I went to make copies of my lesson for my students and on my way back to my classroom, he spoke to me. Now do not forget, I saw this guy all the time but for some reason on that day it was like he was finally revealed to me. I actually noticed him for the first time. You may not believe this, but I never really noticed him before. When he spoke to me my heart fell down to my feet, and I saw the most wonderful person.

He said to me, "You are a fine black woman, too bad you're taken." Wow, I could not believe my ears. I could not believe that someone like him noticed me. He was handsome, intelligent, educated, and had his own vehicle and home. I had to pinch myself to see if I was dreaming. Finally, a man that had something going on for himself, I thought. When he said that, he smiled and walked away. Now I was on a mission. I had to get to know this man.

From that day forward we started seeing each other, and we were growing quite fond of one another. As I began to spend time with him though, I found out that he was married and separated from his wife. That was my clue to exit stage right, but Oh no! I was very attracted to this man, and all I could hope for was that he wanted to be with me. My God, I knew better. What was I thinking? It had been such a long time since I met a man like him. He was not addicted to drugs and he was not homeless. I knew what to do but I did not want to do it. I was fighting a losing battle. His heart was still with his wife as it should have been, and he had two small children. He was an excellent father and I could see that he adored them. I never got an opportunity to spend time with him and his children because he did not want them to know about me. I must admit that I felt bad about that, but later, I began to understand that this man did me a favor to not allow me to get close to his children.

I could sense that he was beginning to have strong feelings for me, although, he would deny it. He had some very peculiar ways and he could be very unkind. Not too many people cared for him on the job because he was very proud, and they saw that this guy was not good for me and that he would eventually break my heart. I saw the good in him because that was what I wanted to see. Although on many occasions he would do things to hurt my feelings; however, we always managed to hug each other when he came by to visit me. That was our ritual. When he came through the door, there I was to greet him with open arms. He would hold me with so much passion and affection as though he was in that place that he did not want to ever leave. Yet it was nothing for him to push me away with his unkind words when I did not do or say what he thought was appropriate. It got to the point where I began to feel uncomfortable; it was like walking on eggshells all the time.

When I became ill, John came one time to the hospital to see me. He would call my home on occasion, but for the most part, I did not have too much contact with him. It was not until I returned to work that he started talking to me again. He was trying to make things work with his wife and I understood that. We still remained friends and he would come over to my house every now and then. I knew that there could never be a future for us. I guess I just wanted to still have that closeness. I would find myself thinking; *I miss the hugs but not the hurts*. So I felt compelled to write this book about my mishaps with men, and the desire I had to encourage and motivate other women to do differently; desiring and striving for more in their relationships.

I finally came to my senses and became very serious about the calling on my life, and for which, was about to get ordained as an Evangelist. I wanted John to come to the ordination. I spoke to him about coming to the ceremony but he did not appear to be interested. Then I got the nerve to ask him a question, and this was the question that let me know exactly what our relationship was made of. I asked him for his address so that I could send him an invitation to the ceremony. He did not say much but I could tell that the question bothered him. Then I really got a spirit of boldness in me and asked him why he could come to my home, but I was not invited to his. Well, that did it, ladies. He dropped me like a sack of hot potatoes. The next day, when I got home from work, I listened to my answering machine where he left me a message. He told me that he never wanted to see me again and he practically accused me of trying to stalk him. I have never stalked anyone in my life; I would not know how. I was prepared for that day. God allowed me to let this man go in my heart and believe it or not, I was just fine. I never saw John anymore, although he had called to see how I was doing. I have not been in a serious relationship since 2002. I am no longer lonely. I am very focused and determined. I am at peace with my singleness.

My relationships truly taught me a valuable lesson. They taught me not to allow myself, ever again, to become entrapped just for affection. It taught me to follow my spirit. It is much more accurate than a carnal mind and a lustful heart.

I dare say, that many women today are in relationships that they do not know how to let go of. Their fear of being alone is stronger than having the courage to be alone until that special beau comes along. Being in love is a beautiful mystery; one that is welcomed, without a single thought of failure and heartbreak, but the journey is quite often traveled.

Yes, I want to be hugged, but I am tired of having to deal with the hurts just to receive a hug. I am tired of compromising my values, God's values, just to say I am in a relationship that is not going anywhere.

I was blessed because God, in His infinite wisdom, mercy and love for me, delivered me from what could have been both a spiritual and physical death. Unfortunately, there are many women who do not and will not receive such deliverance. They are either laid out in a dirt bed, too proud to speak, or they are so miserable that they often wish they could be dead.

When you come to the realization that you deserve to be happy and God wants to give you happiness, you will allow your life to line up with that divine purpose that God has predestined you to live.

"For I know the plans I have for you," declares the Lord, "plans to prosper you and not to harm you, plans to give you hope and a future" (Jeremiah 29:11, NIV).

Let's get ready for the hugs, lots of them, but let's also prepare ourselves to avoid the pitfalls that the enemy will set for us. Personally, I get tired of being part of the negative statistics—alone and settling. Don't you? We are fearfully and wonderfully made, we are not junk; therefore, we do not belong with junk. You are a jewel, and God wants to send you friends and a mate who appreciates the value of a jewel. So be encouraged and look forward to the beginning of God's best for you (smile).

"You do not have time for a bunch of drama in your life. If it is not on stage or a movie screen, it should be unacceptable."

Chapter 10
Questions To Consider

1. What do you miss most about each past relationship?

2. What don't you miss about each past relationship?

3. What did you learn from each past relationship?

4. If you are in an unpleasant relationship, what keeps you from letting this relationship go? Why?

Read the poem on page 114.
Share this study guide as a group project.

Chapter Eleven

The Gold, The Glitter
And The Girls

Now ladies, if you have a special man in your life, or a grown male relative or maybe even a good male friend; pass him this book after you have read the book entirely. I wrote this chapter especially for the men. I do not want the men to feel left out by any means. This chapter will be a blessing to the men because it will expose the areas that many men fall in and will aid them in avoiding this trap again, if they take heed. I am not trying to act as though I have all the answers on the subject; but I do know that by divine revelation, observation, and experience I can effectively and efficiently speak on the subject.

In the beginning, when God created man, He gave him dominion over everything, and with that dominion came responsibilities. When God saw that man could properly handle this, he gave him a wonderful gift—A WOMAN!

The Lord God said,

> *"It is not good for the man to be alone. I will make a helper suitable for him." So the Lord God caused*

the man to fall into a deep sleep, and while he was
sleeping, he took one of the man's ribs and closed
up the place with flesh. Then the Lord God made a
woman from the rib he had taken out of the man, and
he brought her to the man. The man said, "This is
now bone of my bones and flesh of my flesh; she shall
be called 'woman,' for she was taken out of man"
                    (Genesis 2; 18, 21-23, NIV).

So it was God who gave man possessions, status and a sexual partner. It was a good plan because God made it. If the author of Genesis were to wrap up the creation story with this statement it would have been called the eighth day, because eighth for God means a new beginning, and he probably would have started all over to clean up the mess that man made.

The gold, the glitter, and the girls are the three areas that the man has allowed himself to fall prey to the enemy. As I mentioned in the first paragraph, God intended for man to have possessions, and be respected by his peers, and the woman in his life. If a man lacks in these three areas, his ego or manhood can literally be destroyed. What was intended to guide man has turned into a curse which now drives him to defeat and total destruction. It is because of these three G's that our men cannot stay focused on serving God, his family, or his community. He is often so busy chasing after wealth, power, and sex that he becomes a puppet for the enemy to use in executing his plan.

Don't you know that when you offer yourselves to
someone to obey him as slaves, you are slaves to the
one whom you obey—whether you are slaves to sin,
which leads to death, or to obedience, which leads
to righteousness? (Romans 6: 16, NIV)

I am saddened by the mentality of many men in our western society, even those who proclaim to know God. It is also my observation that the male ego has been overly inflated and misused. God intended that his ego be a driving force to provoke him to fulfill his role as a protector, provider; nurturer, and lover to his life partner (helpmate) and children. Instead, and too often, the role of the man has been misdirected due to the dismissing of godly values, and principles. Furthermore, men, successful or otherwise, tend to be impractical when it comes to deciding who to get involved with. They are fixated with how large a woman's butt and breasts are, and how freaky she is in the bedroom. What they should be concerned about, is her family upbringing, and her stability—emotionally and financially. A man needs a woman to be emotionally supportive and responsible for her own financial matters before joining bank accounts.

"They are fixated with how large a woman's butt and breasts are, and how freaky she is in the bedroom. What they should be concerned about, is her family upbringing and her stability—emotionally and financially."

It has been stated in numerous media apparatuses that men cheat and they often use and misuse women. This boggles my mind because he came from a woman and life comes from him through a woman, but he still does not fully understand the value and much-needed role of her presence. So as a result of this abuse and misuse, many women have studied and mastered the game that many men play and have learned to beat them at their own mastery. That is a woman who no longer desires the love, affection, and protection from a man. Her entire objective is to control, manipulate, and deplete him completely of his resources much like the men who have subjected her to the same treatment.

Now then, my sons, listen to me; pay attention to
what I say. Do not let your heart turn to her ways or

stray into her paths. Many are the victims she has
brought down; her slain are a mighty throng. Her
house is a highway to the grave, leading down to the
chambers of death (Proverbs 7: 24-27, NIV).

As a whole, women are tired of the concubine harem mentality that men have exhibited for generations; that it is all right to have your cake and eat it too. Although having many wives and lovers may had been a practice during the Old Testament biblical days and may still exist presently for some religions in Third World and Middle Eastern nations, which are based on the laws of their culture, that practice is not lawful for the majority of the world nor is it scriptural, under the New Testament teachings. But because the man has chosen to operate outside of the spiritual principles that God has sanctioned to keep the world in a peaceful and tranquil condition, the consequences have been grave. To start, the institution of marriage has become almost a complete mockery. There is literally little or no faith in the marriage union. The family has lost its strength due to single—mom headed homes because so many men do not think it is necessary to help raise his kids. Yet he so enjoys making them. This causes the woman (who feels very desperate sometimes) to pursue another love interest in order to get provision for her and her children. In this endeavor, she often chooses the wrong man, and innocent children are subjected to emotional, physical, and sexual abuse. What is really sad is whether or not any of these men show interest in the children at all. They just want to lay with the woman.

Our communities and churches are plagued with violence, deprivation and sexually transmitted diseases because it lacks the positive, male-role models needed to lead them. The churches are plentiful—one in almost every corner. They have charismatic ministers and faithful members—but in many of them, the only thing missing is the true Spirit of God; because they strive towards having the largest membership, the nicest buildings, and the fattest pockets, while the needs of the community often go unmet. The people who are mainly suffering are the women and children who have been abandoned by the man. The same man who so passionately made love to the woman, impregnated her, and then left her and his children to 'fin' for themselves, and at the mercy of other predatory men, community agencies, and self-indulgent ministers.

Now please allow me to switch gears for a moment. I would like to share with you a story that has a very sad ending, and it is very personal for me, because it is about someone that I loved very dearly. Again, I do not want to disclose his real name (because he is deceased) out of respect for his memory, I will call him Will. As I share this with you, I want you men, to seriously take heed to what I am trying to convey to you.

Now, Will was a man of the world, and he was tall, dark, and handsome. I believe that he could have had any woman he wanted, because he often had any woman that he set out to get. Will handled a lot of money and could pay cash for anything he desired. I mean big-ticket items, such as cars and large screen televisions. He worked everyday and took great pride in his work, but his greatest pride was in his side—hustle that he ran, and I must say, it was ran very efficiently. He did not bother anyone because he was just that kind of guy. He had a vice—in fact a couple of them—smoking and drinking. It was his drinking habit that hindered him from going any further than he did in life. He really enjoyed doing it and was not about to get any help for this addiction.

Will always thought he had the upper hand on every one and everything. He even declared many times that he was God because his lifestyle and his manipulation and control over people made him feel that way. He probably thought he was invincible, especially when it came down to running his business. He was very generous though. If you asked for anything he would give it to you. Just do not ask when he was drunk. He would make you owe him favors.

Yes! Will had the good life. He was the big man at his job and people respected him. It was nothing for him to have a big wad of money in his pocket, and when you needed it he had it, but of course it came with a price. This was the lifestyle of Will, and he did this for many, many years. If you were to ask him if he was enjoying life he would say, "Hey, life is good." Well, as you know, all good things come to an end, and Will was about to go out not knowing what hit him.

Will also thought he had it going on with the women; I am sure that you can understand why he would feel that way but one day he met someone that had a venom he was not going to be able to handle. He had a woman who was the worse of the worst She came in with a scheme that he could not even figure out. She quit a good paying job and moved herself and her two sons into his home. This woman was running the show, and she wasn't even his wife yet. She would not allow him to help his mother financially and she disrespected his mother; Will had been a blessing to his mother for many years. The woman even turned his adult children against him because she was so controlling when they came to visit. Oh yes, he met his match. Now the final act to the scheme is what placed the icing on the cake. She got pregnant just to force him to marry her. She had her claws on him all the way now, and there was no escape.

Her sons were not made to respect him and the beautiful little girl she had with him did not respect him either. His daughter called him by his first name, never Dad, and tried to boss him around.

He gave this woman everything, and if she did not get her way, she would deny him sex. Let me pause for a moment, men. Are you getting the picture? This went on for a while until the night his empire came tumbling down.

As I mentioned earlier, her sons were not made to respect him, especially the oldest one. This young man did not work and he used drugs. He did not respect his mother either. Well, one night this young man came home, and he was high, and Will was drunk. So neither one of them was thinking straight. The young man challenged Will, and one thing led to another, and the young man was carried out in a body bag and Will was carried out in handcuffs, and he never saw his empire again.

Will died in prison a poor man and his wife took everything. He was buried in a cardboard box. It was the most pathetic sight you could have ever wanted to see. Before he died, he rested in his mother's arms in the infirmary. I do not know what Will's last thoughts were; but I hope he repented for allowing the gold, the glitter, and the girls to ruin his life. This is not only Will's story, but this is the saga of many men; because your weakness lies in your crouch, and greed and power is tagging very closely behind.

> And he told them this parable: "The ground of a certain rich man produced a good crop. He thought to himself, 'What shall I do? I have no place to store my crops.' Then he said, 'This is what I'll do. I will tear down my barns and build bigger ones, and there I will store all my grain and my goods. And I'll say to myself, 'You have plenty of good things laid up for many years. Take life easy; eat, drink and be merry.' But God said to him, 'You fool! This very night your life will be demanded from you. Then who will get what you have prepared for yourself?' This is how it will be with anyone who stores up things for himself but is not rich toward God" (St. Luke 12: 16-21, NIV).

Men, do not allow yourselves to become entangled in your lustful desires for the flesh because like Will, the force will overtake you. It is time to set a standard for your lifestyles and just like I admonish the women to be selective, I admonish you more so. You should be very selective as to whom you lay with, because it is your seed that creates a nation. Make it your aim to find a wife, and not have several sexual partners. The media and men of the world have taught you that it is cool to have a lot of sexual partners without responsibility, but they do not address the consequences behind giving away your most precious gift, your seed; thus creating bastard children. Please do not take offense at this term 'bastard.' I mean no disrespect, but I will explain what I am bringing to light. Webster defines the term, bastard, as a person born of parents not married to each other; of illegitimate birth or of uncertain origin.

The Word of God says,

> *"If you are not disciplined (and everyone*
> *undergoes discipline), then you are illegitimate children*
> *and not true sons. Moreover, we have all had human*
> *fathers who disciplined us and we respected them for*
> *it. How much more should we submit to the Father of*
> *our spirits and live?" (Hebrews 12: 8 and 9, NIV)*

A child needs a father. If you are not there to reinforce the nurturing the mother is trying to enforce, then you are treating your child like an illegitimate child; a child that has been abandoned by his/ her father and lacks origin. There is no discipline from your hand; no support shown to the mother of your child in creating balance in the child's life—as a male role model. If God's lack of intervention suggests that we would be considered bastards, what do you think your absence suggest? Even if you are present, the disrespect you are showing your child's mother by not marrying her and making your child legitimate, still incites that your child is a bastard according to Webster's definition. If she wasn't good enough to marry, why did you lay with her? We know the answer to that. She was a sexual interlude, but you laid down two and got up three. Maybe you made a mistake being with the wrong woman. But by the time you get to the woman you are suppose to be with, you will be all used up. Just like there are a lot of messed up men, there are a lot of messed up women and you have to keep your guard up too.

There are women who live to destroy a good man's life because she is miserable. She lurks in the homes, the churches, and the community. She is rich, she is poor; she is big, and she is small. She appears to be everything you want in a companion but she comes with baggage and she has already worked out her plan for your demise. The more ambitious you are and the more you like to flash your money, beware. She is manipulative, controlling and greedy and she has no concept of love because she is driven by her desire to have that stronghold on you. That kind of woman knows what to jiggle and what to wiggle to get you.

Hey, whether we like it or not, from the beginning, God intended for man to be the head. I am not trying to imply that they all do it well, but that was the divine plan. God didn't give this responsibility to the woman. The woman is the lifeline to him. She is the neck that holds up the head. Her role is very vital to his existence and should not be belittled, as it so often is. If we look at the human anatomy, the neck possesses the lifeline to the entire body (jugular vein). It is especially, important for the brain. If for some reason that Jugular vein is severed, life stops. The neck also possesses several bones that are strong enough to hold up the head. It is responsible for the mobility of the head. The neck is to the head what the woman is to the man. She is his lifeline. She holds him and influences and assists in his most important moves (decisions). When she is no longer present in his life, the man's quality of life is altered. Every area of his life is affected. A study was conducted where the life span of a man was measured. They found that a married man of one wife, that is, in a monogamous, committed relationship lived longer and had a better quality of life than a man that was single and noncommittal.

Understand this; I didn't write this chapter to bash the men. I wrote it to address the seriousness of a real issue. The issue of the breakdown of the most wonderful love God created, the love between a man and a woman and how it affects other relationships. As stated previously, the man does play a vital role in its destruction. Yes, the woman has her role to play in all of this; but remember, women are responders. They react to how they are treated, and what you are seeing today is the response to the ill treatment many women have endured—the anger, being overly independent, the lack of affection, and short tolerance for nonsense and yes, even trying her hand at "playin'" the game. Oftentimes, the man is present but has played the game for so long, that he takes a very passive position in providing for, loving, and nurturing his family. She was not originally given that responsibility. She is waiting for the man to take his rightful place in the marriage, the family; the community, and the church. Then, and only then, will she be able to fulfill her designed purpose to and for the man to help meet his goals and aspirations. She will stand by his side, not behind him and not in front of him, as they both witness the beauty of their original purpose to come full circle.

Also, I wrote this chapter because I realize that men are victimized too. They sometimes allow themselves to get involved with the wrong women because they need their egos stroked. You see, a man is only as good as the amount of money he makes; his ability to care for and protect his family, and satisfy his woman sexually. If he feels he is lacking in any of those areas, then he feels inadequate. Just like men can sense when a women is feeling bad about herself, so can women sense when a man is not at his best. A good woman will stroke and nurture a man's ego and try to build him up. A bad woman will take advantage of him during his weakness and utilize the opportunity to destroy him.

Men, God gave you your ego and He is the one that you should go to, for your reassurance. Your self—worth is not based on your ability to perform sexually, but somehow you have been taught to believe that lie! Yes! He wants you to take care of your families, and protect them. Yes! He wants you to work and enjoy what you do for a living, and yes he wants you to satisfy your wife (one woman); but all of that is possible only when you place God as the head of your life and seek Him for guidance. You are only as adequate as He allows you to be. You can do nothing right in your own strength.

> I am the vine; you are the branches. If a man
> remains in me and I in him, he will bear much fruit;
> apart from me you can do nothing (St. John 15: 5, NIV).

Men, it's time for you to take your rightful place as the head of the household and as the head in your community and churches. Stop being stumbled by your lustful ways and sexual indiscretions. We (women) need you, we love you and we appreciate you; at least I can say we want too. Yes, there are some bad apples in the bunch but there are so many good ones too. Let the woman take her place, and that is to stand at your side and help you with all of your endeavors. We do not want to share you with other women and take the risk of destroying a generation due to AIDS and other sexually transmitted diseases. We do not want to raise your babies by ourselves. We need you to guide us and provide for us. We love our men, but we want our men to be men and make us proud. You are the pillar that holds up God's creation and the light to the path of life.

Stop the foolishness, do not be suckered in by the gold, the glitter, and the girls. Instead, take a stance and live life right and follow the ordinance of your creator and hold fast to your dignity and integrity. It's because of you that all life exists. So please, do not take it for granted.

The gold, the glitter, and the girls; these three G's have been man's weakness since the beginning of mankind. He's been chasing them. It is time to stop the madness and look at the signs of the time and realize that whether you want to believe it or not; we have a real problem on our hands. I can go on and on in naming the problems and concerns, but you already know what they are. Ask yourself this question. Do you care? If you do, then begin with you—CHANGE! This goes for both men and women. Take an active role in reconstructing what we've made a mess. Charity begins at home—in your home and then it will spread abroad. Then it will begin to have the snowball affect, and then our families, communities, and churches can be saved. The gold, the glitter and the girls—stop letting them destroy our world. Peace!!

"We do not want to share you with other women and take the risk of destroying a generation due to AIDS and other sexually transmitted diseases. We do not want to raise your babies by ourselves. We need you to guide us and provide for us. We love our men, but we want our men to be men and make us proud. You are the pillar that holds up God's creation and the light to the path of life."

Chapter 11
Questions to Consider

1. How important do you think having a positive and godly role model in the home is for the family today?

2. If you are a husband, do you still woo your wife? Even after ten years?

3. If you are a single man, do you think it's all right to have multiple sex partners? If yes, is it all right for the woman to do the same?

4. Is it all right to father a child and place the responsibility for caring for the child solely on the mother, and possibly on another man?

5. When you sleep with a woman (unmarried) do you ask yourself if she gets up pregnant is this the woman you want to be the mother of your children? Is she worthy of marriage?

6. If you answered no and you still proceed, what's wrong with this picture?

7. Do you consciously and actively teach your boys the importance of treating a woman with love and respect?

8. Do you consciously and actively treat the women in your life (mother, sister, female friends, etc.) with love and respect?

9. Please prioritize the following items from one to five; be honest—job (career), God, children, ministry, wife.

I Miss the Hugs, But not the Hurts

I miss the hugs, but not the hurts.
I miss the ups, but not the downs.
I miss the smiles, but not the frowns.

I miss the hugs, but not the hurts.
I miss the talks, but not the silence.
I miss the walks, but not the running
away from you.

I miss the hugs, but not the hurts.
I miss the joy we shared,
but not the moments of despair.
I miss the ray of hope we had,
but not the lack of trust that's there.

I miss the hugs, but not the hurts.
I miss the peace, but not the fear.
I miss the hugs, but I do not miss you!
I miss the hugs!

Written by: Dr. Tunishai A. Ford

God's Plan for Your Mate Selection

Everyone longs to give himself or herself completely to someone, to have a deep and committed soul relationship with another, to be loved thoroughly and unconditionally. But God says, "No, not until you are satisfied, fulfilled and content with being loved by *Me* alone, with giving yourself totally, unreserved to *Me* alone.

I love you, My child, and until you discover that only in *Me* is your satisfaction found, you will not be capable of the perfect human relationship that *I* have planned for you. You will never be united with another until you are united with *Me*; exclusively of anyone or anything else; exclusively of any other desires and longings.

I want you to stop planning, stop wishing and allow *Me* to give you the most thrilling plan existing; one that you cannot imagine. *I* want you to have the very best. Please allow *Me* to bring it to you.

Just keep your eyes on *Me*, expecting the greatest things. Keep experiencing that satisfaction knowing that *I am*. Keep learning and listening to the things *I* tell you. You must be patient.

Do not be anxious. Do not worry. Do not look around at the things others have. Do not look at the things you think you want. Just keep looking up to *Me*, or you will miss what *I* want to give you.

And then, when you are ready, *I* will surprise you with a lover far more wonderful than you could ever dream. You see, until you are ready, and until the one *I* have for you is ready *(I am working even this minute to have both of you ready at the same time)*. Until you are both satisfied exclusively with *Me* and the life *I* have prepared for you, you won't be able to experience the love that exemplifies your relationship with *Me* and this is perfect love.

And, dear one, *I* want you to have this most wonderful love; *I* want you to see in the flesh a picture of your relationship with *Me*, and to enjoy materially and concretely the everlasting union of beauty, perfection and love. *I am your God, and you are my child.* Believe it and be satisfied."

—Author Unknown

I MISS THE HUGS BUT NOT THE HURTS
STUDY GUIDE/ JOURNAL

I hope that this book has been a tremendous blessing to you, and you will tell others about your experience, but the journey is not over. It is time to take a step forward in realizing your full potential, but in order to do this, healing, recovery, and discovery must take place. I have added this study guide to aid you in that task. I hope that it will be helpful to all of you—may God bless you and may you discover that you too . . .

—Miss the Hugs but Not the Hurts—

Chapter 1:
Lord Why Do I Keep Attracting the Wrong Men

1. Reflect on your past or present relationship and ask yourself what attracted you to this person? Make a list. Now be honest with yourself.

2. How long did you stay in a relationship that you knew you were unhappy in and why?

3. Are you still with that person? If not, what compelled you to leave?

4. Are you ready to release the hurts of past and present relationships? If you are, recite this prayer:

"Father,
in the name of Jesus,
I come to you asking for forgiveness
for allowing myself to get involved
with the wrong person.
I was anxious and didn't wait on you
to send that perfect helpmate for me.
I ask that you cleanse me and give me a fresh start.
Allow me to guard my heart and stay focus on
the things you placed in my heart to do.
Thank you, Father,
Amen."

Chapter 2:
Respect Yourself

1. What is respect? Can you honestly say that you respect yourself?

2. Do other people respect you? Identify the reasons you believe they do or don't.

3. Respect is earned—what are you doing to ensure that you continually earn respect or not earn respect?

4. How does God feel about self-respect? See if you can find a scripture that supports how he feels about self-respect.

Chapter 3:
Can You Stand to Be Alone?

1. Do you have strong feeling of despair because you feel alone and lonely? Are you suffering from depression?

2. Write down five activities that you would like to get involved in(i.e., going to the spa, etc.).
   a.
   b.
   c.
   d.
   e.

3. Reflect on your daily activities and then ask yourself what you do to keep yourself busy so that you won't feel lonely. If you don't do anything, consider adding the activities listed in number two to your life to fill the void.

4. Is your loneliness or alone feeling due to a lack of spirituality? Do you feel that you are searching and in need of developing a closer relationship with God?

5. If you answered 'yes' to question four, please recite this prayer aloud.

"Father,
I am feeling lonely and alone.
I know that it is not your will that I feel this way.
I long to have that emptiness filled
and I've tried filling it with things
that couldn't fulfill me.
Please come into my life and
reveal your love to me in a special way.
I need you to fill that void in my life and
I expect you to do it.
Thank you, Father.
In Jesus' name,
Amen."

Chapter 4:
Looking Content

1. Are you anxious to have a man in your life? If you answer, yes, slow down and begin appreciating the time that you spend with yourself and others.

2. In waiting for that person you long to be with, you should be working on being content. Allow me to offer you some suggestions.

   a. Daily pray the prayer you just read in chapter 3.

   b. Daily adorn yourself—make it your business to always look your best (i.e., hair, makeup, colors, fashion).

   c. Surround yourself with people who are in healthy, nurturing relationships.

   d. Get a hobby and / or find activities that you enjoy doing.

   e. Write down the characteristics you would like to present to your mate and work on them.

Chapter 5:
The Woman in the Mirror

a. It is very important to work on inner beauty before we work on the outer beauty. Unfortunately, we live in a society that doesn't place a lot of emphasis on character. I believe that in order to attract that ideal person, you have to work on being the best that you can be. Remember, "Pretty is as pretty does." Identify at least three character flaws you know you must work on.

b. Do you believe that these character flaws can hinder you from getting or keeping your mate?

c. Are you a woman who feels that outer adornment is all a woman needs to attract a man? If you strongly feel this way, where did this come from?

d. Do this exercise—tell one friend about a character flaw you want to work on and ask him or her to help you work on it. Consciously work on changing this for fourteen days and after the fourteenth day ask your friend if he or she has noticed a change in you in that area. Work on it until that flaw is gone. Success to you!

Chapter 6:
Preparation Is not Lost Time

1. What are you doing to prepare for your mate (i.e., lose weight, etc.)?

2. Have you asked God to show you the areas you need to work on to get ready to receive what he has for you?

3. Make God a major participant in your preparatory process. By doing this, you will sense that this process is not solely yours to do and there is another responsible partner that is greatly concerned about your progress.

Chapter 7:
You've Got to Be the One to Get the One

1. How often do we find ourselves mentally making a list of the characteristics we want to see in our dream guy or girl? Then when we meet someone, that mental pictures pops up and we find ourselves comparing them to that mental image. This mental imagery is totally unfair, especially if you don't measure up to that which you are expecting from someone else. Identify on a piece of paper the characteristics you are looking for in your mate.

2. Identify on that same piece of paper the characteristics and qualities you have to bring into the relationship.

3. Are your prerequisites realistic?

4. Re-examine your expectations and ask yourself, should they be lowered or brought up a notch or two?

5. Look at the person in the mirror—Are you that person too?

Chapter 8:
Yesterday is Dead—Today is Born

1. Letting go of the past is sometimes one of our greatest challenges. Our past mistakes have been known to haunt us and keep us trapped in an abyss of hopelessness, but it's time to look forward to the future and take an active role in it. Let's begin by denouncing negative feelings and thoughts we may have about ourselves. Begin to look inward for the strength, courage, and direction we need to capture and live happily in the future. Wr i t e down past mistakes that have been haunting you and hindering you from going forward.

2. If these mistakes revolve around a manor woman, openly admit your part and forgive yourself. Openly admit their part and forgive them.

3. If you are struggling with unforgiveness, let me give you a revelation. Forgiveness is for you. It releases you from a great spiritual strap that can lead to sickness and disease, such as depression and cancer. Allow me to walk you through an exercise that will assist you in this plight.

Write down the names of the people you
are having difficulty forgiving.

Repeat this affirmation:

*I forgive
(say the person's name)
by faith and I choose to love them.
My love is greater than the hurt and pain
they inflicted on me and I release them.
I'm making a conscious decision
to go forward in my life and
I'm not taking these past relationships
with me.*

Note:

You can also say this in the form of a prayer by
the affirmation with 'Amen'.

Tear and throw away the piece of paper,
smile, and get on with your life.

Chapter 9:
It's Your Time

1. Well, you have identified what you want in a man/woman. You know what you need to do to change and you've step out of the past into forgiveness and healing. Now it's time to execute a game plan for greatness. Begin to see yourself as the most wonderful person in the universe and desiring to share yourself with the world. Begin working on those things you have always desired to do(i.e. *lose weight, start a business, go back to school, write a book, etc.).* Remember it's your time utilize it to the hilt. Don't waste the greatest commodity God has given you. Write down your goals—realistic ones and short term, and actively and faithfully start working on them.

2. Tell a good friend what you are doing. This will help with accountability. If someone else knows you are trying to accomplish something, (i.e. losing weight, etc.) you will be less likely to cheat.

Chapter 10:
I Miss the Hugs But Not the Hurts

1. What do you miss most about each past relationship?

2. What don't you miss about each past relationship?

3. What did you learn from each past relationship?

4. If you are in an unpleasant relationship, what keeps you from letting this relationship go? Why?

Re-read the poem on page 112.
Share this study guide as a group project.
God Bless!

Chapter 11:
The Gold, the Glitter, and the Girls

1. How important do you think, having a positive and godly role model in the home is for the family today?

2. If you are a husband, do you still woo your wife? Even after ten years?

3. If you are a single man, do you think it's all right to have multiple sex partners? If yes, is it all right for the woman to do the same?

4. Is it all right to father a child and place the responsibility for caring for the child solely on the mother, and possibly on another man?

5. When you sleep with a woman (unmarried), do you ask yourself if she gets up pregnant is this the woman you want to be the mother of your children? Is she worthy of marriage?

6. If you answered 'no' and you still proceed, what's wrong with that picture?

7. Do you consciously and actively teach your boys the importance of treating a woman with love and respect?

8. Do you consciously and actively treat the women in your life (mother, sister, female friends, etc.) with love and respect?

9. Please prioritize the following items from one to five. Be honest! Job (Career), God, Children, Ministry, Wife

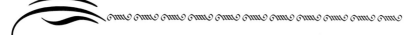